The Theatre of Frank McGuinness
Stages of Mutability

The Theatre of Frank McGuinness
Stages of Mutability

Edited by Helen Lojek

Carysfort Press, Dublin

A Carysfort Press Book

The Theatre of Frank McGuinness. Stages of Mutability
Edited by Helen Lojek

First published in Ireland in 2002 as a paperback original by
Carysfort Press, 58 Woodfield, Scholarstown Road,
Dublin 16, Ireland
© 2002
Copyright remains with the authors

Typeset by Carysfort Press
Cover design by Alan Bennis

Printed and bound by Leinster Leader Ltd
18/19 South Main Street, Naas, Co. Kildare, Ireland

This book is published with the financial assistance of
The Arts Council (An Chomhairle Ealaíon), Dublin, Ireland

ISBN 9781904505013

Caution: All rights reserved. No part of this book may be
printed or reproduced or utilized in any form or by any
electronic, mechanical, or other means, now known or
hereafter invented including photocopying and recording,
or in any information storage or retrieval system without
permission in writing from the publishers.

This paperback is sold subject to the conditions that it
shall not, by way of trade or otherwise, be lent, resold,
hired out, or otherwise circulated in any form of binding,
or cover other than that in which it is published and
without a similar condition, including this condition, being
imposed on the subsequent purchaser.

Contents

Introduction   vii
Helen Lojek

Chronology   ix

Crossing Through *Borderlands*
Brian Cliff   1

World War One in *Observe the Sons of Ulster Marching Towards the Somme*
Bernice Schrank   19

Observe the Sons of Ulster Talking Themselves To Death
Kathleen Heininge   25

'This Woman Has Received a Blow That Will Shut Her Up Forever': Frank McGuinness's *Baglady*
Margot Gayle Backus   41

The Masquerade of the Damned and the Deprivileging of Innocence: Frank McGuinness's *Innocence*
Eamonn Jordan   50

Derry Comes to Mid-Michigan: Staging *Carthaginians* at Central Michigan University
Timothy D. Connors   79

***Carthaginians*: Narratives of Death and Resurrection in a Derry Graveyard**
Anne F. Kelly-O'Reilly   92

Directing McGuinness Plays:
Sarah Pia Anderson in conversation with Sharon Braden   108

Watching Over Frank McGuinness's Stereotypes
Helen Lojek   125

Self-Dramatization in the Plays of Frank McGuinness
Joan FitzPatrick Dean   143

Of *Mutabilitie*
Christopher Murray   162

A Director's Perspective on *Mutabilitie*
Michael Caven in conversation with Helen Lojek   175

Contributors   195

Introduction

Frank McGuinness debuted on the Irish dramatic scene with *The Factory Girls* (1982), a play inspired by women in his family who worked in a Donegal shirt factory. Before that he had published only a few scattered short stories and poems. Since then he has produced fourteen original plays, peopling the stage with vibrant, often eccentric, characters in settings from the Renaissance to the present, from Ireland to the Middle East. His prolific outpouring of varied dramas has been greeted with applause, wonder, and frequent puzzlement. Responses to McGuinness's plays have not been as varied as the works themselves, however, and often analyses (including my own) have relied on the author's own pronouncements.

McGuinness is a formidable commentator on his own work. He has been generous about illuminating what are sometimes private references, and he has skilfully helped to prepare audiences for his challenging themes. Authorial though they are, however, McGuinness's views are neither authoritative nor final. This collection of essays, unified primarily by concern with the dramatic writing for which McGuinness is best known, brings together a diverse set of non-authorial perspectives. It seeks not to illustrate a single approach to McGuinness's work, but to juxtapose discrete voices, different points of view, wide-ranging philosophies, and varied methodologies. Some of the pieces have been published before but should be more accessible reprinted here. Many are new. Some contributors are seasoned responders to McGuinness; some are here publishing work on him for the first time. Commentary comes from theatre professionals and academics in various parts of the English speaking world. The volume is intended for both general readers and specialists. The juxtaposition of heterogeneous contexts and approaches is deliberate, and the anthology format preserves the reality that the voices responding to this playwright are as varied as the voices of his characters. The primary assumption of this volume is that in the dialogue about McGuinness the final word has not yet been written, much less spoken. The collection aims to invigorate the dialogue, not to lower the curtain prematurely. It situates itself in that rich domain before conclusion, knowing that there are other voices, other points of view to be heard – and hoping that readers will add their own accents to the conversation.

In a proper world, expanded discussion will yield additional productions of plays that deserve a wider audience and fuller exploration of their possibilities. The plays are political not in an *agit prop* sense, but in the wider sense of concern with how humans carry out the eternally challenging task of living, in private and in public. McGuinness's ability to address such issues without being either dour or foolishly optimistic is among the many recommendations of his work. A playwright who can make us laugh while searing our souls is always worth another look.

The pieces in this collection are organized roughly in line with the chronology of McGuinness's work. In a way, then, they illuminate the development of a playwriting career more specifically detailed on the chronology following this introduction.

I am grateful to McGuinness for writing the plays, to theatre professionals who shared their insights, to writers who contributed important new perspectives, and to authors and journals who have granted the right to reprint material. I am equally grateful to Carysfort Press.

Helen Lojek, Boise State University

Chronology

1953 McGuinness born in Buncrana (County Donegal)
1974 BA (Honours) in English Language and Literature, University College Dublin
1976 MPhil in Medieval Studies, University College Dublin
1982 *The Factory Girls*
1984 *Borderlands*
1985 *Gatherers*
Observe the Sons of Ulster Marching Towards the Somme
Baglady/Ladybag
1986 *Innocence*
1988 *Carthaginians*
Times in It
1989 *Mary and Lizzie*
1990 *The Bread Man*
1992 *Someone Who'll Watch Over Me*
1994 *The Bird Sanctuary*
1997 *Mutabilitie*
1999 *Dolly West's Kitchen*
2002 *Gates of Gold*

Crossing Through *Borderlands*
Brian Cliff

> Try to put him in a box and you'll find he has somehow wriggled out of it and gone elsewhere.[1]

Frank McGuinness's drama is very much a matter of the space between – between generations, between identities, between communities. Much as he does not stay 'in a box,' McGuinness fits with neither of the critically defined generations of contemporary Irish playwrights. Born in 1953, he falls between those old enough (like Friel, Kilroy, Murphy, and Parker) to have reached adulthood before the period when First Economic Programme began to affect the Republic and those young enough (like Carr, McDonagh, and McPherson) never really to have known another period.[2] His generational position has a geographical parallel in McGuinness's birthplace in Buncrana, Donegal, one of the three Ulster counties not incorporated into Northern Ireland; McGuinness himself has suggested that growing up in Buncrana left him straddling 'the split between a southern training and a northern temperament.'[3] This split surely contributes to what Joe Dowling, the Artistic Director at the Abbey when it first staged *Observe the Sons of Ulster* (1985), describes as 'the almost schizophrenic sense of duality in McGuinness's work. "If you live in Buncrana," he says, "and you want to go to Derry to the pictures, you have to cross a border and change your money into sterling – and he's made the crossing."'[4]

One need not resort to a regional determinism to see a striking synchronicity between this setting and a body of work in which community figures as a matter of boundaries and divisions, sometimes for the better but often for the worse. In part through its attention to these boundaries, McGuinness's drama is always deeply attuned to community's dangers as well as to its simultaneously persistent desirability, to the 'tension between the forces that divide us from others, thus making us outsiders, and the forces which draw us together, thus bonding us positively and negatively into communities.'[5] This is the dynamic behind *Borderlands* (1984), an early play that dramatizes many of McGuinness's concerns with the paradoxes and ambivalences of community. Many of McGuinness's protagonists share the ability to hold together contraries without forcing a false resolution, an ability that is central to the vision of community in his plays.

Although the open quality of this vision can become a kind of shapelessness when McGuinness's writing falters, it is also essential to his dramatic strengths. These strengths are inseparable from his active use of plurality, within plays like *Borderlands* and *Observe the Sons of Ulster* but also through the stylistic heterogeneity of a career that includes plays as different from each other as *Someone Who'll Watch Over Me* and *Mutabilitie*, or *Mary and Lizzie* and *Dolly West's Kitchen*. As that heterogeneity suggests, McGuinness is a ventriloquist in a philosophical sense well beyond that inherent in his genre; he is essentially a playwright of difference – not just from his audience, but also from himself. Such an emphasis supports the production of a theatrical metamorphosis, one that could begin to redress what McGuinness describes as the 'greatest mistake we have made': 'not that we didn't love our neighbour, rather we don't know them, and that is our continued, mutual choice.'[6] By dramatizing this choice as forcefully as it does, *Borderlands* gives an early focus to his concern with belonging and community.

This concern is part of what Eamonn Jordan has described as McGuinness's theatrical search for 'the existence of many voices,' which Jordan contrasts sharply with Friel's more rhetorical 'search for a 'common voice …'[7] McGuinness has often explicitly described this interest in pluralities; during a 1985 interview, for example, he challenges Seamus Deane about

> the neglect of diversities other than the Catholic-Protestant/Nationalist-Unionist ones in Field Day: the diversities between the needs of men and the needs of women, between the needs not simply of rich and poor, but within the middle class, and of the homosexual and the heterosexual. I feel a sense of comfort about Field Day: it is in danger of repeating itself.[8]

Field Day had rejected *Observe the Sons of Ulster* not long before this interview, and McGuinness may therefore have had a direct investment in this critique. Nonetheless, such a defense of heterogeneity reflects a body of work that more closely resembles a web of intersections than a grid of divisions. This willed heterogeneity has shaped a critical awareness about an 'impatience that abounds in McGuinness's drama, a sense that it is rather late in the day for rehearsing the same old pieties and grievances.'[9] Indeed, rather than simply revising or critiquing national and religious 'pieties' yet again, McGuinness often seeks new forms altogether.

Of the forms of plurality with which he engages, McGuinness's treatment of sexuality seems to receive the most critical attention.[10] At times, in fact, his writing almost appears to treat homosexuality as a matter of course, an approach that may actually be more rather than less subversive. Asked by an interviewer whether he 'wanted to deliberately introduce' homosexuality into his plays 'because of Gay Liberation or because of Irish society,' for example, McGuinness responded bluntly: 'Well, no, because I'm gay actually – it's as simple as that. ... I write about it because I think it's worth writing about and worth exploring but I've written as much about heterosexuality though "cause I find that very difficult and very mysterious and strange.' In the same interview, McGuinness suggests that Ireland is 'not nearly as enlightened as some people would want to imagine but [homosexuality is] certainly not nearly as difficult a subject as it was' when *Innocence* premiered in 1986. With homosexuality neither a synonym for subversion nor entirely assimilated by Irish society, then, McGuinness is a 'gay playwright' perhaps in the sense in which he is a 'political playwright': 'I see myself as a playwright and politics impinges on so many affairs of our lives I cannot avoid that writing plays. But I would no more shy away from [politics] than I would embrace it if you know what I mean.'[11] The approach to community in his plays reflects this position: at once sceptical and engaged, it avoids wholesale ideological commitment but never withdraws into neutrality or into the shelter of quietism.

Observe the Sons of Ulster (1985) is generally treated as a remarkable advance on *The Factory Girls* (1982), a sign of rapid artistic and technical maturation, but *Borderlands*, the play that falls between, shows McGuinness already pushing his art farther and farther. His contribution to the TEAM educational theatre group, *Borderlands* was 'written for performance to an audience of senior second-level students, aged between fifteen and eighteen years,'[12] an experience that McGuinness has described as a lesson in 'survival. The hell with critics, they're nothing compared to a hall full of lively sixteen-year-olds whose attention you have to hold for an hour and a half.'[13] Martin Drury, the director of TEAM, explains in his introduction to the play that *Borderlands* was originally commissioned with the idea that it 'would examine language/the making of language/the uses and abuses of language/language and thought etc.' (B 150). Drury sees this theme primarily in the character of the Guard, who is

> frighteningly real, not in the naturalistic sense, but rather in the direct way he gives expression to the institutional violence and the perversion of language embodied in the Criminal Justice Bill, which was being debated in the Dáil while we toured BORDERLANDS, and which became central to many of the post-play workshops. (B 151)

The broad linguistic theme survives in the final version of *Borderlands* less in the Orwellian sense Drury describes than in the play's careful, sceptical attention to collective pronouns like 'us,' 'our,' and 'we.' This attention, in turn, underpins the play's dramatization of the ways in which communal definitions of identity can disrupt and distort community rather than fostering it, a focus signalled by the title itself.

Borderlands centres on a group of four boys – two Catholics, Rocky and Laser, and two Protestants, Fluke and Scott. Depending on which boy is speaking, they are from Derry or Londonderry and they are, as Rocky tries to explain later in the play,

> pushing this wheelbarrow from home to Dublin. We're collecting enough coins to fill the barrow.
> **Scott:** It's for charity.
> **Laser:** The Third World. (B 179)

Even before introducing Rocky and Scott to the audience – 'Get on with the story. This is not just about us. Bring on the other two' – Fluke and Laser explain that they met at the funeral of a young boy:

> **Fluke:** Sixteen years old. Killed in what is known as the fight for freedom.
> **Laser:** Not his own side's freedom. But the other side's.
> **Fluke:** A traitor to the Protestants.
> **Laser:** And a stranger to the Catholics. So he must be buried alone.
> **Fluke:** This would bring tears to a tombstone. But to cut a very long story short, I met this gazebo at Stephen's funeral.
> (B 158)

At the play's conclusion, Fluke reveals that Stephen was his 'simple, stupid brother, who changed sides and died' and describes him in communal, nearly religious language as 'Everybody's brother' (B 189). Fluke's conflicted sense of allegiance here prefigures *Observe the Sons of Ulster*, where Pyper's loving respect for the dead becomes ensnared with communal expectations. Shortly after they cross the border into the Republic, the boys are confronted by Vonie, the woman on whose land they are trying to camp (without permission). She gets a policeman, the Guard, to evict them, but his violence towards the boys changes her mind and she invites them to stay. The boys promptly reject this offer, turning instead towards home and bringing the play to a close.

Throughout these events, irony and sarcasm are consistently prominent in the boys' voices. This prominence is magnified by the play's frequent violations of the fourth wall. The adolescence of the four boys surely increased the play's appeal to the original school-going audience; at the same time, it provides a realistic basis for their self-conscious sarcasm, one which allows the play to question the boys' relationships to their communities without itself succumbing to sarcasm's self-protective elements. Fluke displays more of this sarcasm than do the others but he may also recognize its limitations, perhaps even grasping the element of truth in Lewis Hyde's maxim that 'Irony has only emergency use. Carried over time, it is the voice of the trapped who have come to enjoy their cage.'[14] The play's acerbic tone becomes apparent almost immediately when, in the seemingly simple act of introducing themselves to the audience, Laser and Fluke, the two most articulate characters, stumble on the name of their 'home':

> **Laser:** We come from this town in the north of Ireland called Derry –
> **Fluke:** Actually, we call it Londonderry.
> **Laser:** Dublin-derry?
> **Fluke:** No way.
> **Laser:** Would you settle for Derryderry?
> **Fluke:** O.K.
> **Laser:** We come from Derryderry. (B 157)

While the almost Beckettian rapid-fire absurdity of this compromise suggests a casual uncertainty about their home, the different versions of 'we' here also dramatize the convictions and assumptions that govern communities' senses of themselves. Through this dramatization, this exchange helps raise the play's questions about the intersection of community and language, an intersection that can become not just a means of self-definition – a name that also functions as a border – but its own kind of trap.[15]

Though veiled by the same sarcasm that seems to highlight it, a sharp awareness of the various communal tropes and euphemisms of their home is shared by all four boys:

Laser: Maybe I'm just being a bit sensitive but I think that remark was a tiny bit provocative to the Catholic element in this happy ecumenical group.
Fluke: No way. Aren't we a shining example to our divided community?
Rocky: Burying religious differences for the sake of the starving millions.
Scott: Four young lads showing their troubled country the way.
Laser: God, aren't we fair great? (B 160)

While insulating *Borderlands* from the potentially treacly clichés of its own scenario (to which the play almost gives in), this ironic scepticism also casts doubt on the viability of the communally determined identities that make their group ecumenical. When the four boys struggle to set up a tent for the night, for example, Fluke strings together another series of phrases that build to a faux-Arnoldian conclusion: 'Alien territory. Different vibrations. Never fear. We shall overcome. Protestant craftsmanship here. Catholic enthusiasm there. Unbeatable combo when they work together' (B 164). In scenes like this, the play's didacticism (which already blends realism and allegory) combines with the consistent voice of the boys to depict them as on the border between recognizing the force of the tropes that have defined their communities and succumbing completely to those tropes.[16] Although hemmed in by their relationships to their respective communities and by the presumptions about identity that sometimes go with those relationships, the boys are not yet locked in place. Much of what follows in the play reflects the boys' struggle to shape identities for themselves rather than merely accept imposed or inherited ones.

These identities are most explicitly defined – by the stage directions and by the boys – in terms of Catholic vs. Protestant. Having identified themselves to the audience in these terms, the first two characters on stage, the Protestant Fluke and the Catholic Laser, quickly proceed to a ritualized exchange of sectarian insults that they present as a necessary introduction:

> **Laser:** Since the insults have already started, could we get them over with quick?
> **Fluke:** Sure, Papist. You want to start?
> **Laser:** O.K. Let's stick to the script, I'll be the Catholic, you be the Prod.
> **Fluke:** No, keep the customers satisfied, keep them guessing, swop. Right, go.
> *Rapid fire delivery*
> **Laser:** Fenian pup.
> **Fluke:** Orange dog.
> **Laser:** Taig.
> **Fluke:** Planter.
> **Laser:** Provo.
> **Fluke:** Paisleyite.
> **Laser:** Left-footer.
> **Fluke:** Right-footer.
> **Laser:** I'm getting confused. Which is which?
> **Fluke:** Keep it going, man. Keep it speedy. Don't think, just shout. Go! (B 156)

Such appellations as these appear at once fixed in their predictability and arbitrary in the ease with which they are switched; like the 'Derryderry' scene, this scene questions the appearance of fixity in the relationships between religion, community, and identity in Ireland. As the play stages this conflict between the fixity and arbitrariness of communal identities, the boys are increasingly caught between pessimism and optimism.

When Laser impatiently questions the relevance of such communal divisions and blames their endurance on sectarianism, the boys begin an argument that is much less playful than their earlier banter. Scott tries to smooth things over by offering the ecumenical truism that 'There's good and bad on all sides, Catholic and Protestant,' but Laser echoes McGuinness as he replies that

> in the north, good and bad don't come into it. Only us and them. Fenians and Orangemen. Take your partner and hate the other side. Love your neighbour? Do you realize what that would mean at home if we actually try to do it? But we won't, because we're scared. We're afraid to know them, let alone love them. And that fear will be the end of us. (B 172)

Despite their superficially shared scepticism, Fluke rebukes Laser's local focus as ultimately distracting and 'out of date ... It's still, yes, boss, no, boss, three bags full, boss, except now it's multinational boss. ... That big word's the master now. We're all natives to it, children, all inferior, Fenians and Orangemen alike.' The sectarianism that Laser sees as the disease itself Fluke sees instead as only a symptom of this larger web of forces; rather than calling for harmony in the name of a shared Irishness, both here and later in the play Fluke sees something like a Foucauldian web of power.[17] Rocky, coming to Laser's defence and resisting Fluke's worldview, charges that, globalization or no, 'there are a damned sight more Fenians than Orangemen in the dole queue' (B 172). This only pushes Fluke to respond dismissively that Rocky is merely 'playing into the master's hands' and to ask a version of the play's central question: 'Stand up for your own. But who is your own? We'll fight that out among ourselves and we'll be so busy fighting we won't have time to fight the new masters' (B 173).

Borderlands never grants any view full authority, and Fluke's rhetorical victory here is as much a matter of his dominant, energetic character as it is a sign of political finality. Still, the play does seem to sympathize with his argument about the impact of economic globalization on local communities, an argument that recalls McGuinness's *The Factory Girls*. The language of this argument pushes the boundaries of the play's governing concerns with 'us' and 'them' away from some of the sectarian assumptions that can dominate discussions of community in Northern Ireland. The play undermines the claims of transcendence or universality implicit in those assumptions by placing them alongside a larger political and philosophical context that opens the door to many more versions of 'us' and 'them.'

The play's physical movement from Northern Ireland into the Republic and back to 'Derryderry' opens this door most directly and allows the play access to the disjunctions between identity and community. When Rocky makes the casual assumption that he and Laser are 'not strangers ... We're still in our own country. We don't recognise the border' between the

Republic and Northern Ireland because 'We're Irish,' for example, Fluke quickly insists otherwise: 'Well, we do recognise the border. Once we cross it, we're not in our own country. Whatever Irish we are, we're not your Irish. We're in the borderlands, Scott and myself' (B 161). By refusing to mistake what should be for what is, and by recognizing these borderlands as both a state of mind and a physical place with political consequences, Fluke may begin to feel his way towards a different basis for community than that with which the boys have grown up.

Fluke is proven only too right that they are caught between communities when Vonie appears and asks another version of the play's central question: 'Who the hell do you think you are?' (B 175). Interrupting the boys' attempts to explain their ecumenical, cross-border charitable mission – and distinctly unimpressed by Fluke's assertion that they are 'Dancing in the borderlands' – Vonie erupts in a fit of impatience that bespeaks a long-simmering frustration with

> collections of your type. We're not completely stupid down here. ... I'm sick and tired listening to your like whinging and whining whenever I switch on the television. I'm fed up hearing what you're going through. I'm sick of checkpoints and helicopters and army jeeps. It's been going on too long up there. One time you might have had my sympathy, but not anymore. Whatever you've got you've brought on yourselves. We've had enough of you. We're tired listening. We're tired of it all. (B 175)

Fluke's pointed response – 'Join the club lady' – is at once flippant and effective not only in taking away her soap-box but also in creating a sardonic community based on rejection (B 176). After Vonie leaves, the four boys fall back to arguing, with Scott and Rocky attacking each other along strict sectarian lines and Fluke returning directly to the language of his earlier argument with Laser:

> Well, Laser? I'm not trying to start a battle, but are people in the south more open and generous? Not always watching themselves or their property. They welcome strangers, eh?

We're not strangers, right, Rocky. We're in our own country. Wrong. We're not. None of us are. (B 176, emphasis added)

As Fluke seems to recognize in his insistent use of first- and third-person collective pronouns here, Vonie's forceful definition of their group as one homogeneous Other creates a more tense group solidarity than had previously been at stake in their playfulness. That earlier solidarity was chosen in spite of their differences from each other and perhaps even in part because of those differences; this solidarity is enforced by their collective difference from the Republic, represented by Vonie and the Guard. As Riana O'Dwyer has argued, this confrontation brings them 'to the realization that neither the Protestant Derry boys nor the Catholic Derry boys are at home in Southern Ireland. They have more in common with each other in terms of shared effort at friendship and shared bereavement than they will ever have with the southerners who regard them as trouble makers.'[18] Particularly for the Catholics Rocky and Laser, their exclusion challenges their understandings of themselves and of their immediate community, as well as of the various relationships to the world at large which flow from those understandings. As part of the play's consistent attention to the instability of collective pronouns, this challenge undermines any reliance the boys might have on a stable sense of community.

Vonie's reappearance with the Guard returns the boys to their contingent internal unity, as they put tit-for-tat suspicions of each other's motives on hold in the face of an external threat. Through this scene and its consequences, *Borderlands* establishes a vision of community in which 'us' and 'them' is relational rather than fixed, a vision that extends Fluke's earlier argument about the dynamics of community and globalization. As subsequent McGuinness plays dramatize in their own ways, such encounters can impel a disparate collection of people to think of themselves as a community, albeit a very contingent one. When Vonie finally recoils at the Guard's brutality and invites the boys into her house, for example, Fluke bitterly rejects her change of mind in just such terms: 'Will you come into my parlour, said the spider to the fly? Not I, not I. No way.

No, no. … But what kind of one are you? What kind of ones are we? You don't know us. We don't know you. Leave it at that. Leave us apart. Close your parlour door' (*B* 184). Vonie may represent the Republic's turning away from the North to the comfort of its own relative prosperity here, but the play's interest in the dynamics of community leads it to emphasize instead the disillusionment and consequent withdrawal of the Northern boys.

Clearly, such communal fault lines are very much a matter of the specific context of Northern Ireland and of the borderlands that are in part a consequence of that state. At the same time, these particularly Irish questions also raise more general questions about the nature and difficulty of belonging. Amin Maalouf has written passionately that 'wherever there is a divided society, there are men and women bearing within them contradictory allegiances, people who live on the frontier between opposed communities, and whose very being might be said to be traversed by ethnic or religious or other fault lines.' These are not, he continues, 'a handful of marginal people. There are thousands, millions of such men and women, and there will be more and more of them.'[19] What, then, does it mean to invoke 'us,' in Northern Ireland, in the Republic, or elsewhere? What is entailed in or expected by community, whether in its particular or its abstract forms? How can community be defined and protected? *Borderlands* dramatizes this questioning attitude towards the uses of community in Ireland primarily through Fluke's scepticism. As the examples above show, Fluke forces different versions of the play's key questions into the dialogue, but not just at the expense of the Catholics or the Protestants in the group. Instead, he forces them almost every time that the opportunity presents itself: 'Who are your own, Scott?'; 'Whose side? What side?'; 'Stand up for your own. But who is your own?' (*B* 167, 173). Acutely sensitive to the entanglement of self-definition with communal identity, Fluke magnifies the play's already intense awareness of the way in which collective pronouns are freighted with meanings – difficult, unreliable, and unpredictable – vastly out of proportion to their size. As a result of this social and linguistic weight, the boys struggle to understand themselves in relation to their communities and to define those relationships in a way that does not leave them bereft of agency.

Near the conclusion, Fluke finally uses a collective pronoun without apparently turning it to sarcastic or interrogatory ends:

> **Fluke:** Grow up. Do that, if you can. ... Your wee dream was shattered. Organise a big march. All on our own. Nobody behind us. Just Catholics and Protestants. There's more to this world than Catholics and Protestants. There's power. It doesn't always wear a uniform, but it's all around us, and we have none of it. Power can push our like aside. ... Scenes with your big policeman, that's our world ...
> **Laser:** I agree we have to change the system that –
> **Fluke:** We are the system. We have to change ourselves. (B 187-8)

Even as he emphasizes structural sources of power here, Fluke gives no sign that 'ourselves' or 'our like' is available for sarcasm or dismantling. This difference marks this passage as perhaps the closest thing to a moral in *Borderlands*, albeit one without many specific prescriptions. Such a pointed, awkward passage offers a reminder both of this play's origins as an educational theatre project and of the necessarily incomplete translatability of dramatic writing. The latter is particularly true of a play like *Borderlands*, which draws on experimental forms to create its own momentary community by engaging the audience directly, an engagement that later McGuinness plays often make through a much more ritualistic framework.

Having offered this small glimpse of communal vocabulary, Fluke and Laser quickly move to a brief but telling moment in which they seem to belong together as much because of their differences as in spite of them. When Laser learns about Fluke's dead brother, he asks

> **Laser:** Why don't you cry for him?
> **Fluke:** Cry for the dead? I'm too busy crying for the living.
> *Laser touches Fluke.*
> **Laser:** O.K.?
> **Fluke:** O.K.

Laser: Sure?
Fluke: Yes.
Laser: You leave me? Never. You won't turn your back on me. You can't.
Fluke: How do you know?
Laser: A dickiebird told me. A very private dickiebird. Only I can hear him. He talks a lot like you, only lower, nearly always under his breath. You have to listen real hard to know what's going on. Someday I'll let you hear him.
Fluke: When?
Laser: A happier time.
Fluke: A better place.
Fluke slowly offers Laser his hand. Laser takes it. (B 189)

In keeping with the apparent simplicity of much of the play and with the difficult questions it has asked, *Borderlands* finally offers this limited but hopeful vision of a future community in the making: 'A better place.' When the play concludes with Fluke and Laser's duelling renditions of 'God Save the Queen' and 'We're On the One Road,' however, as Eamonn Jordan suggests, the boys are repeating 'the clichés of their individual tribe[s] ... but this time the clichés are listed with a new awareness.'[20] Despite the playfulness of this 'new awareness,' the continued presence of the clichés confirms that *Borderlands* attempts to envision heterogeneous forms of community without resorting to a dubiously bland agreeability. Such forms heighten the need to 'change ourselves' that Fluke asserts, a change necessary first to create a community and then to sustain it.

McGuinness has noted a similar interdependency between the individual and the communal in the theatre, where 'the story has been taken from the community at large, and interpreted, given back to it by the story-teller ...' Through such a mutual engagement, he suggests, 'the individual is dependent on the community and the community is in some way dependent on the individual in the making up of this story.'[21] In this view, community is a process and a story that draws on both the individual and the collective; as *Borderlands* depicts it, this story must remain open and its conclusion cannot be predicted.

Rather than a *laissez-faire* act of faith or a retreat into quiescence, however, the play illustrates McGuinness's own suggestion that 'To say "I don't know" is one of the strongest forms of political assertion ...'[22] By positing community as a continual process that leads to a way of belonging rather than to a finite, known identity, *Borderlands* draws on the essential openness of McGuinness's drama to lay a technical and thematic foundation for the plays that follow.

[1] Ray Comiskey, 'Frank McGuinness: A New Breed of Irish Playwright', *The Irish Times*, 2 May 1987, Weekend p.9.

[2] Brian Friel was born in 1929, Tom Kilroy in 1934, Tom Murphy in 1935, Stewart Parker in 1941, Marina Carr in 1964, Martin McDonagh in 1971, and Conor McPherson in 1971. For a recent analysis of modernization in Irish culture, and of the mythic weight of the First Economic Programme, see Conor McCarthy, *Modernisation, Crisis and Culture in Ireland, 1969-1992* (Dublin: Four Courts, 2000).

[3] Frank McGuinness, 'Strange Passion About the Somme', interview with Charles Hunter, *The Irish Times*, 15 February 1985, p.12.

[4] Comiskey, p.9.

[5] Helen Lojek, 'Difference without Indifference: The Drama of Frank McGuinness and Anne Devlin', *Eire-Ireland*, 25.2 (1990), pp.65-66.

[6] Frank McGuinness, 'I am not confident for my country's future', *The Irish Times* 25-27 December 1989, p.8.

[7] Eamonn Jordan, *The Feast of Famine: The Plays of Frank McGuinness* (Bern: Peter Lang, 1997), p.188. Jordan is quoting Richard Kearney's description of Friel from *Transitions: Narratives in Modern Irish Culture* (Dublin: Wolfhound Press, 1988), p.125.

[8] Jennifer Fitzgerald, 'The Arts and Ideology: Jennifer Fitzgerald talks to Seamus Deane, Joan Fowler and Frank McGuinness', *Crane Bag*, 9.2 (1985), p.65. On Field Day's rejection of *Observe the Sons of Ulster*, see Shaun Richards, 'Field Day's Fifth Province: Avenue or Impasse?' in *Culture and Politics in Northern Ireland: 1960-1990*, ed. by Eamonn Hughes (Milton Keynes: Open UP, 1991), pp.142-143, quoted by Elizabeth Butler Cullingford, 'British Romans and Irish Carthaginians: Anti-colonial Metaphor in Heaney, Friel, and McGuinness', *PMLA*, 111.2 (March 1996), p.228.

[9] Claire Gleitman, 'Negotiating History, Negotiating Myth: Friel among His Contemporaries', in *Brian Friel: A Casebook*, ed. by William Kerwin (New York, NY: Garland, 1997), p.234. Similarly, James Liddy sees McGuinness as 'looking for an exit sign from the terms of the tenured Easter 1916 debate. We have been locked into Yeats so much, and his heirs O'Casey and Behan, that McGuinness looks for relief, light and otherwise' ('Voices in the Irish Cities of the Dead: Melodrama and Dissent in Frank McGuinness's *Carthaginians*,' *Irish University Review*. 25.2 [1995], p.281).

[10] A number of critics have focused on McGuinness's work in terms of the disruptive potential of homosexuality within political and national discourses. Fintan O'Toole, for example, argues that McGuinness uses 'the condition of homosexuality itself, as opposed to the situation of individual homosexuals … as a physical metaphor for states of national consciousness …' ('Island of Saints and Silicon', in *Cultural Contexts and Literary Idioms in Contemporary Irish Literature*, ed. by Michael Kenneally [Totowa: Barnes & Noble, 1988] p.32). Although she acknowledges the practical limitations of homosexuality's liberatory, disruptive potential, Susan Harris also argues that McGuinness's plays still offer real hope: 'by making room – however temporarily, and under whatever restrictive conditions – for agency in the process of identity construction, Pyper and Dido suggest a possible strategy for rewriting the script within which they are trapped' ('Watch Yourself: Performance, Sexual Difference, and National Identity in the Irish Plays of Frank McGuinness, *Genders* 28 [1998]:
http://www.genders.org/g28/g28_watchyourself.txt, paragraph 9, accessed 26 June 2001.). In an interview with Richard Pine, McGuinness affirms the idea that 'survival, the dominant theme of [*Carthaginians*], is possible in Dido's case because of, rather than despite, his homosexuality' and remarks that it is 'important to say because one of the earliest sources for the 'voice' of Dido was the music of a pop group called 'The Undertones.' They were very much children of the Troubles' and yet 'they create the most joyous sound of the love of life. They were singing songs in praise of chocolate and girls, and Dido sings songs in praise of chocolate and boys' (Richard Pine, 'Frank McGuinness: A Profile', *Irish Literary Supplement*, 10.1 [1991], p.30). Like Dido, The Undertones

were from Derry and their 1980 album *Hypnotised* parodied their own themes by including a song titled 'More Songs About Chocolate and Girls.'

[11] Frank McGuinness, interview with Jacqueline Hurtley, in *Ireland in Writing: Interviews with Writers and Academics*, ed by. Jacqueline Hurtley, Rosa Gonzalez, Ines Praga, and Esther Aliaga (Amsterdam: Rodopi, 1998), p.68, p.63, p.66.

[12] Frank McGuinness, *Borderlands*, in *Three Team Plays*, ed. by Martin Drury (Dublin: Wolfhound, 1988), p.7. All further citations of *Borderlands* will be given parenthetically as *B*.

[13] Frank McGuinness, 'Speaking for the dead: Playwright Frank McGuinness talks to Kevin Jackson', *The Independent*, 27 September 1989, Arts p.20.

[14] Quoted by David Foster Wallace in Joe Hagan, 'A Thinking Slacker's Rock Hero, Slightly Aged', *The New York Times*, 25 March 2001, Arts p.33.

[15] In *Northern Ireland: A Comparative Analysis* (Dublin: Gill & MacMillan, 1987), Frank Wright analyzes the risks of 'communal deterrence relationships' that draw on a similar dynamic of self-definition (p.149).

[16] Their effort to raise a tent in this scene underscores the allegorical element of the play, readily serving such readings as Eamonn Jordan offers: 'Their initial incompetence captures the general ineptitude of both communities in Northern Ireland to either work together or to agree on the basic techniques of construction, cooperation and communication' (p.9).

[17] Foucault repeatedly describes power through spatial metaphors, as when he suggests that 'Power must be analysed as something which circulates, or rather as something which only functions in the form of a chain. It is never localised here or there' but is instead 'employed and exercised through a net-like organization' (Michel Foucault, 'Two Lectures', in *Power/Knowledge: Selected Interviews and Other Writings, 1972-1977*, ed. by Colin Gordon, trans. by Colin Gordon et al. [New York: Pantheon, 1980], p.98). He writes elsewhere that, 'Just as the network of power relations ends by forming a dense web that passes through apparatuses and institutions, without being exactly localized in them, so too the swarm of points of resistance traverses social stratifications and individual

unities' (*The History of Sexuality, Volume I*, trans. by Robert Hurley [New York: Vintage, 1990], p.96).

[18] Riana O'Dwyer, 'Dancing in the Borderlands: The Plays of Frank McGuinness', in *The Crows Behind the Plough: History and Violence in Anglo-Irish Poetry and Drama*, ed. by Geert Lernout (Amsterdam: Rodopi, 1991), p.105.

[19] Amin Maalouf, *On Identity*, trans. by Barbara Bray (London: Harvill, 2000), p.31.

[20] Jordan, p.9.

[21] Fitzgerald, p.66.

[22] Fitzgerald, p.62.

World War One in *Observe the Sons of Ulster Marching Towards the Somme**

Bernice Schrank

I. Ireland and the Great War

Ireland was only marginally involved in the Great War of 1914-18. Like so much else in Ireland in this period, Irish responses first to the threat and then to the reality of the War were contextualized within the nationalist debate. So for many, the events of 1914-1918 were one more occasion on which to demonstrate either commitment to, or rejection of the Union with Great Britain. In the North, where Unionist sympathies were at least as strong then as they are now, the Ulster Volunteers supported the English war effort by volunteering in large numbers for active service. In the South, all segments of the nationalist movement regarded the war as an English problem, a sideshow that might, as the banner in front of Liberty Hall announced, become 'Ireland's opportunity' for furthering independence. As a result, at least in the South, conscription was opposed, and the English government felt it unwise to implement a draft. Despite this opposition, many Irishmen

---

* *A longer version of this article first appeared as 'World War I in the Plays of Shaw, O'Casey and McGuinness' in* Études Irlandaises, *XVII:2 (December 1992) pp.29-36.*

from the South did in fact volunteer to fight although their numbers never approached those of the volunteers from Ulster, and their sympathies were not necessarily Unionist.

II. Irish Drama and the Great War

These political fault lines are reflected in the treatment of World War I in George Bernard Shaw's two war plays, *O'Flaherty, V.C.* and *Heartbreak House*, in Sean O'Casey's *The Silver Tassie* and in Frank McGuinness's *Observe the Sons of Ulster Marching Towards the Somme*. In his first play about the War, *O'Flaherty, V.C.*, Shaw turns drama to the purposes of recruitment, attempting to convince Irishmen of the South to fight against Germany even if it means siding with the English. In his second play about the War, *Heartbreak House*, he changes focus, writing as a totally Anglicized Irishman assessing the impact of the war entirely in terms of its effect on the English ruling elites. Like *Heartbreak House*, O'Casey's *The Silver Tassie* belongs to the post-War European literature of disillusion. Even so, O'Casey dramatizes the War, at least in part, from the perspective of the Dublin slums, as critical of Irish working-class participation in this conflagration as he was critical of Irish working-class involvement in the Rising and the 'Troubles' in his earlier plays. Writing about Northern Irish Unionists, McGuinness's *Observe the Sons of Ulster* is possibly the most thoroughly Irish of the plays under discussion. In this play, McGuinness dramatizes the ongoing legacy of the War in shaping the political and cultural mythology of Ulster.

Shaw's *O'Flaherty, V.C.* and McGuinness's *Observe the Sons of Ulster* are brackets enclosing a period of about seventy years. Such a time frame provides strong evidence of the persistence of the War in modern Irish memory, even though actual participation was limited. The memories of war are certainly the nucleus of the emotional life of Kenneth Pyper, the main character in McGuinness's work. Late in life, as Pyper relives his war experience once more, it becomes clear that McGuinness's interest is less in memorializing the sacrifice of Ulster soldiers at the Somme than in dramatizing the ways by which historical events become absorbed into, indeed made subservient to, the dominant ideology, in this case Ulster Unionism. For Pyper and, by extension, for other Unionists, the influence of the War continues to be felt in the present.

In examining these plays, it will be apparent that my intentions are threefold: 1. to illustrate the sensitivity and responsiveness of Irish drama to major European events; 2.to indicate the influence of place in shaping the presentation of these events; and 3., somewhat contradictorily, to suggest the diversity and unpredictability of Irish literary responses to major European events.

[...]

V. The View from the North: 'Observe the Sons of Ulster Marching Towards the Somme'

In *Observe the Sons of Ulster Marching Towards the Somme* (1985), Frank McGuinness, born in Donegal, creates a play that treats the War from the perspective of Ulster. Using non-realistic techniques, McGuinness creates an old man, Kenneth Pyper, through whose dramatized memories the events leading up to the massacre at the Somme on July 1, 1916, are presented. Old Pyper recalls his young self, a sensitive isolate who, like all the other young Northern volunteers, finds comradeship and communion with other Ulstermen as they collectively face death. The War is the source of Pyper's profoundest emotions, a shared love of the men for each other, feelings bound by geography, rooted in communal ties of religion and history, and sealed in blood.

When Craig, Millen, Moore, Roulston, Crawford, Anderson and McIlwaine die, Pyper becomes the last living receptacle for their dreams, their values and their goals, connected to them by an emotional umbilical cord that he can never sever. Now an old man, separated from the events of July he depicts by about seventy years, Kenneth Pypr finds his deepest satisfaction in remembering and, in so doing, memorializing the loss of the Ulster Volunteers at the Somme. That their deaths occur on the anniversary of the Battle of the Boyne in 1690 sanctifies them in the eyes of the Ulster community, of which Pyper is now a willing member, and makes them part of the Protestant mythology of blood sacrifice which is just as powerful a political force in Ulster as the Catholic mythology of blood sacrifice is in the Republic.

The events McGuinness dramatizes are deeply tragic. The pastoral nature of the male bonding as Pyper remembers it has a transcendent quality of liberation and exaltation. Yet it is inherently fragile and ultimately doomed. The price of such bonding is life itself. The war that facilitates the loving comradeship of the Volunteers also destroys it.

While the sacrifice of young men in war is tragic, the consequences for the living are also tragic. Of the eight Volunteers who bunk together, only one survives, but he is far from intact. Pyper before the Somme was unconventional, creative, intelligent and outspoken. Pyper after the Somme is a paradigm of the Ulster Unionist with all the limitations that designation conveys. The experience of the War closes his once open nature. To confirm and renew that early bonding, Pyper relives various experiences of his own and of the others. But Pyper's act of remembrance is a complex process in which he not only celebrates the ties of love and of friendship that existed between and amongst the Volunteers, but one in which he accepts the other men's narrow faith and their sectarian beliefs as his own. The bonding is thus more than emotional; it is also political. By reliving his connection with the dead soldiers, Pyper is absorbed into the ideological gestalt of Protestant Ulster. It is part of the tragedy McGuinness dramatizes that the emotional freedom the Volunteers temporarily experience leads to Pyper's lifelong emotional and intellectual entrapment and diminution.

The process by which Pyper absorbs and perpetuates the values of Ulster Protestantism resonates with larger meaning. The play invites extrapolation. As a representative of the Ulster Protestant community, Pyper's fixation on this particular moment not only transforms his life into a death-in-life, but suggests that, with its devotion to death rather than life, the entire community, like Pyper, has grown old and feeble without learning the skills necessary to revitalize itself.

VI. Conclusions

Through their dramatic presentations of World War I, the plays of McGuinness, O'Casey and Shaw convey the differing perspectives of the three Irelands: North, South, and Abroad. In the earliest play by an Irish playwright to deal with the War, Shaw's *O'Flaherty, V.C.*, Shaw focuses on male bonding as one of the rhetorical bases for encouraging Irish Catholics to volunteer for front line duty. Some seventy years later in the most recent play by an Irish playwright to deal with the War, McGuinness's *Observe the Sons of Ulster Marching Towards the Somme*, McGuinness, in a much more lyrical mode than Shaw in *O'Flaherty, V.C.*, returns to the experience of male bonding which is shown to be the source of the finest feelings of which his characters are capable. But whereas Shaw in *O'Flaherty, V.C.* is concerned only with the immediacy of the War and the need to find able recruits, McGuinness, like O'Casey, dramatizes the ambiguities of the War and its impact on the psyches of those who have experienced it. With the exception of *O'Flaherty, V.C.*, the plays are concerned with the socio-political implications of the War: Shaw's *Heartbreak House* concentrates on the dissolution of the old order; O'Casey's *The Silver Tassie* and McGuinness's *Observe the Sons of Ulster*, on the helplessness of a new order to be born.

Works Cited

McGuinness, Frank. *Observe the Sons of Ulster Marching Towards the Somme.* (London: Faber and Faber, 1986).
O'Casey, Sean. *The Silver Tassie*, in *Collected Plays 2*. (London: Macmillan, 1964), pp.1-111.
Shaw, George Bernard. *Heartbreak House*, in *Complete Plays* with Prefaces, Vol. I. (New York: Dodd, Mead, 1963), pp.447-598
-------. *O'Flaherty, V.C.*, in *Complete Plays* with Prefaces, Vol. V. (New York: Dodd, Mead, 1963), pp.123-52.

Observe the Sons of Ulster Talking Themselves To Death
Kathleen Heininge

Within Irish drama of the late 20th century, the use of language as a marker for Irishness begins to shift away from a focus on accents and Hiberno-English, towards a use of language that attempts to actually establish new truths: truths about relationships and alliances, truths about history, truths about memory, and especially truths about identity. Language becomes the very means of change and hope, in drama that has become concerned with the use of language not as signifier of nation but as reiteration of the stories that might be able to change through that reiteration. What is 'true' is no longer shaped by someone else's language, but by the incantatory retelling and recasting of stories in versions particularized by individuals. The words themselves become a means for an imposition of identity. Language is not only the tool, but also the subject for discussion and performance. Whereas some others, including Tom Murphy, Christina Reid, and Enda Walsh, have concluded that language does indeed change at least the perception of truth, Frank McGuinness, in *Observe the Sons of Ulster Marching Towards the Somme* (1985), concludes that language cannot always succeed in its efforts to create a new reality. A play in which eight men try to come to terms with the events leading up to the Battle of the Somme in France during WWI, *The Sons of Ulster* shows us that language may be able to change personal identity, but it can never change history, desirable though that may be.

J. L. Austin, in *How To Do Things With Words*, distinguishes between two different kinds of speech: that which relates information and that which performs an action. The latter he refers to as 'performative' speech, and he goes on to identify different kinds of performative language. 'Illocutionary' speech acts do what they say they are doing in the moment of speech, such as saying 'I do' in a wedding ceremony and with those words, marrying. 'Perlocutionary' speech acts cause effects as a result of being spoken; shouting 'Fire' in a theatre does not cause the fire, but does result in people leaving that theatre. Illocutionary speech acts perform the action and perlocutionary speech acts lead to an action. Non-performative speech simply relates information, without actually creating or causing actions.

Austin indicates that the performative utterance, an utterance that *does* an action rather than simply *relates* information, will be 'hollow or void if said by an actor on the stage'[1] because it loses its force of performing an action; he claims that such utterances are 'parasitic' upon the normal use of performative language. Irish speech on stage, however, constitutes a performative utterance that is not at all hollow or void, but is very much the kind of performative utterance, the speech act, of which Austin speaks. Austin is correct that in much drama, the utterance is merely mimetic, relating information about a subject in varied ways. Within Irish drama, however, the very enactment of speech establishes identity with each reiteration, thus constituting the performative. The action that is performed is the establishment of identity, and the reiteration of that identity eventually brings about a new understanding of Irishness. As David Cairns points out:

> The struggle to interpellate individuals into particular groups, and thereby into accepting a particular outlook upon life, society, history, goes on unceasingly, de-interpellated from one group and re-interpellated into another, and the means through which this constitution of the subject takes place is through discourse.[2]

He argues that the struggle for power is based upon the struggle to be identified or interpellated, and that power is wielded by those who control the 'discourse' of that interpellation. He also points out, however, that those who manage to control the terms of that discourse often find themselves 'trapped and overcome' by that same discourse. A seizure of the discourse, of the means of interpellation, is a consequent seizure of the narrative, and, as Benedict Anderson understands, 'Identity… because it can not be "remembered", must be narrated'[3] in order for community to be established. The very act of narration becomes a form of interpellation, the speech act that the playwrights in the later part of the century have turned to; community is established and identity can be instated. When the narrative is co-opted, it must be repeated often, as though the very performance of the new narration can have the power to erase the narrative that came before, and can create new meaning, a process of which Victor Turner speaks. He claims that performance 'completes' an experience, and through performance, '"meaning" is squeezed out of an event' and allows for 'penetrative, imaginative understanding'.[4] The repeated expression or performance of an experience will allow the experience to be completed, so that those who witness the experience may glean cathartic understanding: reality is shaped through this completion.

Observe the Sons of Ulster Marching Towards the Somme investigates both of these uses of language. Pyper and the others interpellate themselves according to various truths, trying to arrive at an identity that fits, and trying to seize some control over the situation in which they find themselves. Pyper also attempts to glean new understanding of the events by reliving them, and the narrative frame that is used in the play, with Old Pyper telling the story of Young Pyper, serves to indicate that one telling will never be enough to change the truth. Joan FitzPatrick Dean discusses both of these concepts under the rubric of 'self-dramatization,' arguing that many of the forms of meta-theatricality within the play function similarly (see this anthology). I argue the two uses of language, interpellation and re-enactment, function very differently, although to a similar end: a stipulation of a new understanding of truth.

Interpellation

In situating the play in France before the Battle of the Somme, McGuinness sets his characters up to be forced to explore identity and relationships. The 36th Battalion was comprised primarily of volunteers from Ulster, untrained men who were largely drawn from the Ulster Volunteer Force. The eight men in the play are part of this battalion, and have just arrived in France to fight in the British army. Finding that they are given little direction and no introduction, they don't know where they are to sleep or what kind of training they will be receiving, patiently awaiting some kind of instruction. They have become outsiders, seeking a common ground, united in their sameness against the foreignness of France and the British army, when at home in Northern Ireland they may never have encountered each other; the enemy, as Helen Lojek has pointed out, is external to them, providing a sense of unity where there had been none before[5].

In the section McGuinness titles 'Initiation,' these eight men begin to try to establish a sense of community, seeking through interpellation the hierarchy of relationships. Relying on the things that they have in common, they negotiate identity for themselves as individuals and themselves as a group. The terms for that identity, however, continue to shift, as they 'reinterpellate and deinterpellate' themselves and each other. McGuinness allows the characters to reconstitute their relations with each other, seeking that power over discourse that is denied them in their situation at the lowest rung in the British Army. Binary relationships exist throughout, as both Dean and Riana O'Dwyer[6] note, but shift in import and in meaning. From Irish to British (and then to French), North to South, Catholic to Protestant, homosexual to heterosexual, privileged class to working class, 'top brass' to private, Somme to Boyne, living to dead, man to woman, sane to insane, them to us: all of the relationships are dual but none is static. The positioning begins right away. Each of these relationships is interrogated through interpellation, as if the relationships themselves can be understood best as long as they are articulated.

The visual is instantly proven to be only half-right: when the men attack Crawford because he looks like he is Catholic, he insists that they are wrong, although later we find that he is 'half-Catholic,' to the best of his knowledge. When Pyper demands that they all notice the fineness of his skin, he subverts that fineness with the contamination of blood. When Roulston comes in, Pyper recognizes him as does Craig, but they only see their memory of Roulston as a preacher, failing to see that this is not Roulston's full identity anymore. The visual fails and so they turn to the verbal. The efforts to articulate, however, seem to verify the elusiveness of the delineations that the men are so desperate to reify: as they try harder and harder to stipulate who is on which side, the lines between the sides become more and more ambiguous[7], and the terms for interpellation continue to shift. The determination of which binary will take precedence depends on the individuals: religion (Roulston and Crawford), sexuality (Pyper and Craig), region (Anderson and McIlwaine), or history (Moore and Millen).

Pyper is deemed by the men to be crazy because he attempts to interpellate himself as everything simultaneously. Defying categorization, he adopts both sides of each binary, eluding the efforts of the others to stipulate identity. When Craig first enters, Pyper keeps calling him 'sir,' as though postulating his own inferiority, until Craig reminds him that they are the same rank[8]. But when Millen and Moore enter, Pyper interrogates them as though he were an officer, insisting:

> ... you will learn to conduct yourself with respect, respect for this army, respect for your position in this army, and respect for all other position above you. Since there are no ranks beneath you, you will never be at ease again until you leave this army. Do you understand that clearly?[9]

He is both the position of authority and of subordination, and in his playfulness it is impossible to determine which, if either, position is the 'real' one. Pyper tells the men, 'I have never done a day's work in my life' to explain his 'remarkably fine skin'[10], and yet he tells of nearly starving to death in France because of his poverty, occupying both the position of upper class and that of lower class; again, the truth is difficult to determine, and he appears to be playing at both positions. He establishes himself as Protestant, but tells them an outlandish story about marrying a Papist whore (out of curiosity). The conceit of the story brings into question both his Protestantism and his sexuality: he clearly takes neither seriously. He smokes, and he doesn't smoke. He babbles about being 'Fit for dying. Fit for the grave. Fit for pushing up the daisies'[11], and then babbles about the rightness of the war they are there to fight; both stances seem to be mocking, and it remains unclear what he truly believes. In positioning himself everywhere, he positions himself nowhere. As Eamonn Jordan notes, 'With role playing, it is easier to distinguish between accepted, imposed, rejected, misunderstood, residual and emergent versions of self'[12]. The men determine that he is a 'mad bastard'[13], confused by the alternating loyalist and defeatist rhetoric that comes from his mouth. Moore tries to admit Pyper to the ranks of the others, saying at one point, 'Even Pyper has admitted that he's one of our own kind'[14], but Pyper eludes that identity, and the men are ill at ease with him.

By the third section, 'Pairings,' the interpellation of identity appears to be somewhat cemented. On leave in Ireland, the men have paired up and attempt to resolve the issues that they each feel will allow them to face their impending deaths. Pyper, the sculptor, has paired with Craig, who challenges him to reconcile his duality. Pyper, saying that he is 'Flesh. Stone. David. Goliath'[15], insists that he cannot create, that he can only destroy. He remembers his time in France, and The Whore who is dead because of him, telling Craig:

> I couldn't look at my life's work, for when I saw my hands working they were not mine but the hands of my ancestors, interfering, and I could not be rid of that interference. I could not create. I could only preserve. Preserve my flesh and blood, what I'd seen, what I'd learned. It wasn't enough.

> I was contaminated. I smashed my sculpture and I rejected
> any woman who would continue my breed.[16]

He tells Craig that he joined the army so that he could have the last laugh at his ancestors, who made him 'sufficiently different to believe I was unique, when my true uniqueness lay only in how alike them I really was.'[17] He cannot escape the many dualities in his life: he is like *all* of his ancestors, not just some of them, having incorporated all the qualities of the Irish in Ulster; the duality itself is tearing him apart (as it tears Ireland apart), and he alone cannot be interpellated. Even his rejection of that duality fails him, however; he comes from his ancestors and cannot avoid that, but just as he believes he has terminated his line, unable to recreate himself, he finds that Craig himself admits, 'I am you'.[18] Even the duality of creation occurs in Pyper: he is from and he has become. Significantly, however, Pyper, the one who refuses interpellation, is the only one to live.

The other characters, however, albeit conflicted, are more easily interpellated. Although their relations shift, they remain within the confines of the categories that they have established in a way that Pyper seems to avoid. Millen and Moore, clearly established as friends, attempt to work out their fear of death by crossing and re-crossing a bridge; they are both working class, Protestant though somewhat secularly so, and lack the contradictions inherent in the other men, making Moore's terror more poignant. Crawford and Roulston, more sincerely religious and devout, are both in France to redefine themselves, as are many of the characters (see Dean). These two unite in their contempt of the other men, believing at first that they are both above the nonsense perpetuated by Pyper especially. Only when Crawford dares to humiliate Roulston by brawling in the church does Roulston realize that he is not actually the next Messiah, and thus each is reconciled to the slaughter they anticipate. Anderson and McIlwaine, Belfast thugs, go to the Field to re-enact the celebrations of the Twelfth of July, unhappy at missing the events that are so dear to their Protestant hearts. The ambiguity that lies in them is their desperation to let the lambeg drums drown out the noises that fill their heads otherwise, the noise of fear and death, and the sense that the drums are inadequate to the task that awaits them on their return to France.

The interpellation of authority figures large in this section. Judith Butler insists that the hegemonic speaker position is essential to the position of interpellation, that only someone with authority can actually interpellate identity, but that this is not necessarily so within the performative. In the performative, in language that performs an action, the individual who speaks is allotted agency simply *because* of the use of language, and she suggests that the use of language by a figure who lacks authority points out 'how what [language] creates is also what it derives from elsewhere'.[19] In the meta-theatricality of the men's performance of authority, then, McGuinness is questioning the position of the men's ability to interpellate themselves at all.

One of the ironies within McGuinness's choice of the Somme as the setting of his play lies in the position of the soldiers within the hierarchy of the British army, an army that is both foreign and national to these men. Various historical theories suggest different implications behind this fact.[20] Some feel that the UVF had already provided some semblance of training for its men, and so the army could take advantage of men who were not entirely ignorant of battle conditions; others feel that the UVF was targeted for the battle as an act of political murder: although the eventual Union was thought to be at least partly a reward for these lost lives, the suspicion remained that the British were attempting to mitigate the 'problem' of having an illegal Irish group remaining in power once the Union had been achieved. Most theorists deny such forethought, however, concluding that the results of the battle were simply due to terrible planning and to a lack of proper training. As there was little time to prepare the troops for the battle, the training consisted primarily of how to use a gun and how to obey orders unquestioningly. The order that was given was to stick to the plan given, under every circumstance, without consideration of whether or not the plan was a good one. The plan was most notably not a good one.

Better-trained soldiers might have been able to recognize that the plan was unworkable, and would have adapted; rather than running straight into the German guns through open fields, for example, they would have taken cover along the sides of the fields; rather than adjusting the gunfire further forward in prescribed increments that presumed advance, the British gunners would have held their aim at the place where the actual fighting was; rather than assuming that the earlier bombing had destroyed the German forces, leaving the territory safe for advance, there might have been some reconnaissance that could have told them that an open attack was unfeasible. There are many possibilities, according to war historians, but in general two things are agreed upon: the Battle of the Somme represents the greatest defeat in British history, resulting in 400,000 casualties, greater than those sustained by the British in the Korean, Boer, and Crimean wars combined; and the blind obedience of the forces helped lead to the decimation of the 36th Battalion.

McGuinness establishes the lack of training in the first scene, when there is no one to tell the new recruits what to expect or how they will be trained. They must establish their own authority. Clearly the authority of which the military is the epitome is called into question here, perhaps reflecting the colonial situation itself. The volunteers for Ulster went ahead and obeyed the very authority that they mock so relentlessly, despite their awareness that they are heading for death in doing so. They mock the authority in their relations with each other, in trying to order each other around (each of them having a hand in it at some point in the play), in mocking the Battle of Scarva (Anderson trying to 'direct the play' and growing frustrated when they don't adhere to his direction), in mocking the Easter Rising and its results. The men try to establish a new cycle of authority with their words and with their play. In 'Initiations,' the men keep mistaking each other for figures of authority, unable to recognize the authority that they are somehow seeking. Moore and Millen, discussing their imminent return to France, note that the top brass is the only thing that can get them to return, as the brass is the ultimate authority: 'If they order me to fall?' Moore asks, and Millen tells him, relentlessly, 'You fall.'[21] But later, Moore rejects that dynamic, and attempts to assert his own authority, recognizing that the authority of the top brass is just as inadequate for him as the lambeg drums are for McIlwaine.

> **Moore:** You'll never lead me again. I'm on my own here, you're on your own there. That's the way it should be.
> **Moore:** You did, I did, they did.
> **Millen:** Top brass?
> **Moore:** No such thing. Top brass are supposed to give orders. You follow orders. But orders are only orders when you follow them.
> **Millen:** If you've stopped following orders, stay where you are.
> **Moore:** I haven't stopped following orders. I've started giving them.
> **Millen:** Who put you there?
> **Millen:** You want me to leave?
> **Moore:** No. (*pause.*) Wait for me.
> **Millen:** Why should I? You seem to think I know nothing.
> **Moore:** You know enough.
> **Millen:** I don't know you.
> **Moore:** Who led me? Who saved me?
> **Millen:** Who?
> **Moore:** Thanks.[22]

In establishing himself as the new authority, Moore becomes a stranger to Millen. The words, however, clearly fail, in that all the men still attend to the words that come from authority, the orders from the 'top brass' which send them out to war. While they may have managed to save themselves before the larger battle, their very deaths have been interpellated by the 'top brass,' that figure of authority, obviating all other interpellations that they have tried to make with and about each other. The Elder Pyper also seems to recognize this, as he says at the beginning: 'In the end, we were not led, we led ourselves.'[23] The only one of the eight who lives is Pyper, who is reliving it all again, against his will. He is the one who mocked the very act of interpellation, refusing to be interpellated himself and so placing himself in every position, in each binary. The Elder Pyper, however, at the end of the play, has reconciled himself to one reality, to one truth, that of Ulster.

Reiteration

The frame of the play is the narration of the Elder Pyper, who is forced to re-enact the events leading up to the battle for a reason that he does not understand. Reluctant, he protests, 'Again. As always, again. Why does this persist? What more have we to tell each other? I remember nothing today. Absolutely nothing.'[24] Outraged by the need to relive it all again, he recognizes the power that words will have over his memories, over the truth:

> I do not understand your insistence on my remembrance. I'm being too mild. I am angry at your demand that I continue to probe. Were you not there in all your dark glory? Have you no conception of the horror? Did it not touch you at all? A passion for horror disgusts me. I have seen horror. There is nothing to tell you. Those willing to talk to you of that day, to remember for your sake, to forgive you, they invent as freely as they wish. I am not one of them. I will not talk, I will not listen to you. Invention gives that slaughter shape. That scale of horror has no shape, as you in your darkness have no shape. Your actions that day were not, they are not acceptable. You have no right to excuse that suffering, parading it for the benefit of others.[25]

He knows that the very reiteration of the story will give it shape, will simply allow it to be true in a new way, and he refuses to give it that power, knowing that the horror was complete in itself, opposing efforts to make sense of the story. His refusal to participate, however, must also call into question his perspective: What is he trying to do? How reliable is his memory? What does he believe will change? He worries about the reliability of others' memories, of their invention, but he knows that there is no need to invent. He recognizes that with each retelling, the truth becomes more diffuse and impossible to access, but although he hates the idea of giving the story shape, in his blindness it is all he can do. The only thing he can see is the ghosts of those he was with in France. He can no longer see the pink sky, and he tells Craig, 'I died that day with you'.[26]

Although we don't see the battle itself, it remains the subtext for the entire play; the layers of meaning in the play cannot be accessed without a consideration of the history. The Battle took place on July 1, 1916, a date which is fraught with meaning to the Irish. July 1, the anniversary of the Battle of the Boyne (although the current calendar puts it as July 12), is seen by the men as particularly fortuitous, since they hope that history will repeat itself and give further cause for glorious celebration and sash-wearing. The mock Battle of Scarva that the men perform, during which Pyper trips and King James wins, hints that the battle to come may not turn out as they would wish, and implies that the reiteration of the story can indeed change the outcome, or at least the interpretation of the outcome. The Somme also took place only months after the Easter Rising, the story of which McIlwaine recounts as pure mockery: some 'Fenian' named Pearse 'walked in to post a letter and got carried away and thought it was Christmas',[27] and ended up being shot by his own disgusted mother. Pyper asks where McIlwaine got this version of events, and McIlwaine tells him that Roulston told him; Roulston mentions that the best facts were made up by McIlwaine, and McIlwaine is pleased by the admiration of his creativity. Not only does this scene represent an attempt to narrate the story in more palatable terms, revising history, but it also establishes the clear difference between the Northern and Southern concerns: The North is effectively distanced from the South. The irony of using this setting comes, of course, when we consider that when so many of the UVF were killed in the Somme, the union between Britain and Ulster was fairly cemented, according to many, and the relationship with the Republic would never again be one of complete trust and unification. Thus, at least for the results of the Somme, Southern concerns and Northern concerns were inextricably entwined.

While others have discussed the meta-theatricality of the play (including Dean and Jordan), few have discussed the element of prayer in the play. Although the play begins by setting up the re-enactment, it ends with a prayer, the epitome of all performative speech acts, as Fintan O'Toole, discussing Tom Murphy, notes:

> A survey in 1974 found that 97 per cent of Irish people prayed at least once a day, and 45 per cent said that they prayed for material reasons, for protection from illness, for comfort and prosperity. Even fifteen years after Ireland started to become a modern industrial society, the magical notion that one's lot in the world can be transformed by the speaking of certain words remained deeply embedded.[28]

O'Toole goes on to say that words, for Murphy, might be used 'either to maim or to heal, to kill or to cure. Partial, selective revelations are used as weapons to hurt others, and only a full, cathartic exorcism of past secrets can have the effect of changing things and making a new wholeness possible.'[29] The catharsis allows for a mutability of existence that is not otherwise afforded, but those 'partial, selective revelations' are the very things that Pyper fears will give the 'invention' shape. He is thus unsure whether a repetition of the story will maim or heal, kill or cure.

The irony of course is that the prayer is, as we know from our history, absolutely ignored.

> God in heaven, if you hear the words of man, I speak to you this day. I do it now to ask we be spared. I do it to ask for strength. Strength for these men around me, strength for myself. If you are a just and merciful God, show your mercy this day. Save us. Save our country. Destroy our enemies at home and on this field of battle. Let this day at the Somme be as glorious in the memory of Ulster as that day at the Boyne, when you scattered our enemies. . . .[30]

The reality that the prayer attempts to mitigate is relentless; despite Pyper's insistence that the Somme has metonymically become all of their rivers, the river that will take them home, (an insistence that has certainly come full circle since the beginning of the play), the worst of their fears are fulfilled. His friends are killed horribly. Craig exhorts him to survive, and Pyper does live, but it is questionable whether or not he survives. Both the dramatic audience and Pyper's audience know that the prayer is pointless and that death awaits them. The day will be anything but glorious in the memory of Ulster, and its associations with the Boyne (including the date) are unfortunate at best. Words are proven to be unreliable and fallacious, not at all presenting a new reality. The ultimate form of Irish performative language fails in its ability to redefine reality.

Two factors potentially mitigate that consideration of prayer as failed performative. The first is that McGuinness has carefully crafted the prayer to be subjunctive: '... if you hear the words of man, I speak to you this day ... If you are a just and merciful God, show your mercy this day'. Pyper's request is contingent upon something of which he has no clear concept. If the words were purely performative, then they might imply that, in the failure to answer the prayer, there is no God at all. However, this is not the only prayer in the play. Pyper had vowed never to return to France, but 'If I did go back, I asked that I be struck blind. I made a covenant, and I survived.'[31] He did return, voluntarily, and his covenant was indeed honoured. This is the prayer that seems to have been granted, as the Elder Pyper speaks of his lot in life; he did not get to be the hero and die on the field that day, but 'Darkness, for eternity, is not survival'.[32] He cannot be said to have survived when he is refused the illumination of his own identity through the interpellation that heroism might have allowed him. Performativity has its limits: while some individuals may have been re-interpellated, refusal of that interpellation is possible. Ultimately, history cannot be revised, try though one might through reiteration of the narratives of history.

[1] Austin, J. L., *How To Do Things With Words*, (Cambridge: Harvard University Press, 1962), p.22.
[2] Cairns, David and Shaun Richards, *Writing Ireland: Colonialism, Nationalism and Culture*, (Manchester University Press, 1988), p.16.
[3] Anderson, Benedict, *Imagined Communities: Reflections on the Origin and Spread of Nationalism*, (London and New York: Verso, 1983), p.204.
[4] Turner, Victor, *From Ritual to Theatre: The Human Seriousness of Play*, (New York: Performing Arts Journal Publications, 1982), 13.

5 Lojek, Helen, 'Watching Over Frank McGuinness's Stereotypes', in *Modern Drama*, XXXVIII:3 (Fall 1995), p.353. Reprinted in this volume.
6 O'Dwyer, Riana, 'Dancing in the Borderlands: The Plays of Frank McGuinness', in *The Crows Behind the Plough: History and Violence in Anglo-Irish Poetry and Drama*, ed. by Lernout-Geert (Amsterdam: Rodopi, 1991), p.99.
7 Dean, p.91.
8 McGuinness, Frank, *Observe the Sons of Ulster Marching Towards the Somme*, in *Frank McGuinness: Plays 1*, (London: Faber and Faber, Ltd., 1996), p.104.
9 ibid, p.108.
10 ibid, p.109.
11 ibid, p.111.
12 Jordan, Eamonn, 'Metatheatricality in the Plays of Frank McGuinness', in *Theatre Stuff: Critical Essays on Contemporary Irish Theatre*, ed. by Eamonn Jordan (Dublin: Carysfort Press, 2000) p.196.
13 McGuinness, p.136.
14 ibid, p.121.
15 ibid, p.150.
16 ibid, p.164.
17 ibid, p.164.
18 ibid, p.164.
19 Butler, Judith, *Excitable Speech: A Politics of the Performative*, (London: Routledge, 1997), p.17.
20 Schneider, Ulrich, 'Staging History in Contemporary Anglo-Irish Drama: Brian Friel and Frank McGuinness', in *The Crows Behind the Plough: History and Violence in Anglo-Irish Poetry and Drama*, ed. by Lernout-Geert, (Amsterdam: Rodopi, 1991), pp.79-98.
21 McGuinness, p.160.
22 ibid, p.168.
23 ibid, p.100.
24 ibid, p.97.
25 ibid, p.97.
26 ibid, p.99.
27 ibid, p.175.
28 O'Toole, Fintan, *The Politics of Magic: The Work and Times of Tom Murphy*, (Dublin: Raven Arts Press, 1987), p.63.
29 ibid, p.63.

[30] McGuinness, p.196.
[31] ibid, p.110.
[32] ibid, p.98.

'This Woman Has Received a Blow That Will Shut Her Up Forever': Frank McGuinness's *Baglady**

Margot Gayle Backus, University of Houston

In 'The Politics of the Possible', Kumkum Sangari describes Gabriel García Márquez's *One Hundred Years of Solitude* as encoding the mutual construction and interpenetration of the colonizer's historical temporality with that of the colonized. She writes:

> The narratives are obsessed with ... time and derive a special intensity from prolonging stagnation, oppression, decay. On a political level the stagnant time in *One Hundred Years of Solitude* is imposed by a determining history that puts Latin America out-of-date, keeps it in thrall, fixes it in another time. Stagnant time is both indigenous time *and* alien time, in the sense that it is *re*-imposed by foreign domination. Further, such linear time is also embedded in Macondo as the history of European intrusions in some form, and so as its *own* history, there is no such thing as pure or uncontaminated time. It is significant that the concurrent or circular time of Macondo is not only invaded or interrupted by gypsies who bring alchemy, but also exists in dialectical relation with

This article first appeared as part of Chapter Seven ('Perhaps I May Come Alive': Mother Ireland and the Unfinished Revolution') of Margot Backus's The Gothic Family Romance: Heterosexuality, Child Sacrifice, and the Anglo-Irish Colonial Order. *Durham, N.C.: Duke UP, 1999.*

several entries of linear time. Thus the banana company builds a separate enclave within Macondo, fences off circular time in order to exploit it. Linear time is as 'impure' and as oppressive as circular time.[1]

As Sangari points out, there is no such thing as pure or uncontaminated time in *One Hundred Years of Solitude*. The *wish* for such a pure temporal space outside history is a metropolitan precept, imposed and re-imposed by foreign domination. The association of the mother with a pre-Oedipal time of pure and uncontaminated bliss is itself tainted through the implantation into the colony of a capitalist symbolic order within which both 'the woman' and 'the colonized' are constituted as impure 'sites of nature' that are supposed to produce and nurture both children and surplus value. The imposition of English notions of 'pure' exchange value, constituted in opposition to 'contaminated' use value associated with self-maintenance and the production and nurturance of children, produces repulsion against the body of the mother and, indirectly, against the body of the child, where once the body would itself have constituted the 'space outside time.'

The constitution of the child as a gendered object offered up within the settler colonial family as a means through which to extend a colonialist symbolic order is figured, in Sangari's analysis as well as in much of Irish literature, as incest. Sangari speculates that 'if circular time is a metaphor for historical inevitability, then it is important to notice that it does come to an end. Pilar Ternera perceives incest as a cyclic retardation of linear time: "the history of the family was a machine with unavoidable repetitions, a turning wheel that would have gone on spilling into eternity, were it not for the progressive and irremediable wearing of the axle."'[2] In Sangari's analysis I find a model that accounts for the way in which otherwise inexorable systems, such as those that replicate sexual abuse within families or colonial hierarchies, might, over generations, wear down through the accumulated resistance to which their repetitions give rise. The colonial machinery of subject production under such exploitative conditions wears like an axle, as Gabriel García Márquez suggests. While the periodic breakdown of such family systems is, in real life, sporadic and asynchronous, Márquez's intuition that the larger political and economic systems that such family systems collectively uphold must also inevitably spawn their own contradictions is enacted allegorically within each of the texts that I discuss [elsewhere in *The Gothic Family Romance*]. The 'fall' of the Big House depicted in modern Irish novels represents the inevitable end result of a 'wearing of the axle' that occurs at the site of subjectivity itself. This site 'wears' because the means by which the subject is accommodated to society by their nature provoke resistance and friction and because the intra-subjective and historical orders this process of subject formation seeks to make congruent themselves, over centuries, wear and grind away at each other.

In his one-act play *Baglady*, Frank McGuinness provides an allegorical representation of the trajectory that such a wearing of the axle might take. An extended monologue that McGuinness says 'tries to suggest that an individual is not a fixed entity, but always fluid,'[3] the play premiered in 1985. The play's central figure, the Baglady, is reminiscent of the Tarot figure 'the Fool.' Like the well-known Fool of the Ryder Tarot deck, the Baglady carries a mysterious sack. Like the Ryder image, she represents a figure stepping into a historical/spatial void. As do Pyper [in *Observe the Sons of Ulster Marching towards the Somme*] and Dido in *Carthaginians*, two other fool figures from McGuinness's oeuvre, the Baglady represents the discontinuity of the 'self' and the simultaneity of past and present in the constitution of the subject.

In *Baglady*, for the first time McGuinness directly challenges stable constructions of gender as a binary code. In *Observe the Sons of Ulster*, McGuinness critiques the social production of 'masculinity,' as the main character transgresses against masculine coding in ways that clearly amount to a form of (unsuccessful) political resistance. But in *Baglady*, gender itself is thrown into question. According to McGuinness's stage directions, the Baglady 'wears the heavy clothes of a farmer, rough trousers, dark overcoat, boots,' and 'she is feminized only by a grey scarf protecting her head, covering her hair completely.'[4] McGuinness seems to want the audience to experience a moment of uncertainty concerning the actress's gender. Moreover, from the first moment of dialogue, the Baglady is continually paralleled in her monologue by male figures who are clearly herself. Her first lines are: 'I saw someone drown once. I was carrying them in my arms. When I looked behind me, there was nobody there' (73). The figure the Baglady carries in her arms is herself, as well as the illegitimate son that she drowns. The gender of the figure is specifically withheld here.[5] In the next section of monologue, the Baglady sings: 'Who's at the window, who? Who's at the window, who? A bad, bad man with a bag on his back' (73). The 'bad, bad man' who threatens to carry the Baglady away *is* the Baglady, as well as the Baglady's father. The bag on his back identifies him with her, and the action of carrying her away refers back reflexively to the image of the Baglady carrying someone whom she watched drown. Identity continues to proliferate reflexively throughout the monologue in a manner which at once suggests that all subjects in patriarchal cultures have fully internalized the characteristics of both genders and that the Baglady has internalized her oppressor (the father who raped her and whose child she bore) and his oppression lives on, in the present, within her.

The factors silencing the Baglady include the false belief that the past is 'over and done with' – a belief that represents an internalized colonization of time as well as space, because the Baglady's inability to *confront* her past, for fear of punishment in the present, prevents her from liberating herself from the past's impact on her present – and the culturally constituted confusion between her own memories and experiences and the narratives of others. She holds up the five of clubs and muses:

> The five of clubs. A bad card. Don't worry, it's over. It's youth. But it stands for suffering, because it means sorrow….It happened long ago. Somebody did something and you did. Did whoever it was tell you to say nothing, or did you imagine their voice was your own? When you tried to tell eventually did nobody believe you, so you stopped believing too although you saw it all happening? (79-80)

The Baglady's narrative is overlaid with the fairy-tale narrative of the queen of hearts, who also had a son. 'He was taken. The queen left her country in disguise as beggarman, searching for her son. Every time she came to a place where she might find him all she found instead was the same answer. Your son is dead, his father killed him. She couldn't say my son is my father and my father is my son. She couldn't say it, but it was all she possessed, the truth' (80). This passage suggests a re-reading of Yeats's *Kathleen ni Houlihan* allegory, in which the mother (Mother Ireland), a disinherited queen in the garb of a beggar, seeks after sons sacrificed not by her but by the colonial father, who demands the perpetual sacrifice of sons, his own and those of the colonized Other. Here, the father begets and sacrifices the body of his son on the brutalized body of his colonized daughter. The line 'your son is dead, his father killed him,' may be read as an indictment of Ireland's literary fathers, who, dressed in drag as 'Mother Ireland,' have projected the child sacrifice intrinsic to the colonial order onto Ireland and Irish mothers, as well as a broad burlesque of the dilemma of Our Lady, who, impregnated by her heavenly 'Father', bears him the son whom he forsakes and kills.[6]

In the figure of the Baglady, McGuinness conflates the silent *mater dolorosa*, the grieving figure of Mary that came to prominence in Ireland in the wake of the famine, with Mother Ireland, to construct an archetypal mother who figures Mary and Mother Ireland as silenced incest survivors and also represents both the literal injuries sustained by all incest survivors and the figurative injuries sustained by women within the Irish social order. Like [Yeats' play] *Purgatory* and the other 'burning Big House' texts, *Baglady* plays out another possible variation of the breakdown of a Burkean system of cultural and economic replication. As does *Purgatory*'s Boy, the Baglady embodies the final link in a chain of historical causality that she does not comprehend and can no longer contain. Like so many of the children in the narratives I examine in this book, the Baglady is left 'holding the bag' for the transgressions of her forebears; her suicide represents the ultimate triumph of the father over the daughter. Indeed, it constitutes by extension the ultimate triumph of the Oedipal configuration, which exhibits at all moments the passionate desire to suppress and silence, to render up the body of the female as perfectly and uncontestedly material. Yet the death of the Baglady and her child also exacts the final and (within a patriarchal and misogynist society) the only revenge that the daughter can take against the father to whom she belongs as property by Oedipal logic and by Irish law. Through the destruction of her biologically female body, the Baglady removes from her father and her society the means by which they have marked her out as a discursive space on which all of society may write but that may never be claimed for her own use. Above all, however, the drowning of the Baglady represents the end point of an unconscious quest backward toward the site of an injury that was, retroactively, discovered to be fatal.

The violent emergence of the past into the present is represented in McGuinness's use of Tarot symbolism, through which the Baglady divines both her past and her future, only to discover that they are identical. Tarot imagery is invoked through the Baglady's reading of a series of playing cards, in the systematic references to the four elements, and in the play's ritualistic invocations of the subject positions 'Mother', 'Father', 'Daughter', and 'Son' as the Baglady reads the cards.[7] Her reading of cards, along with her ritualized references to burying, drowning, burning, and suffocation (the constitutive symbolic elements of the Tarot are earth, water, fire, and air), violently conflate the past and present. Through imagery associated with historical forms of punishment for witchcraft (the crushing of witches under enormous rocks, a form of live burial, was favoured in Scotland; hanging, a form of suffocation, was preferred in England; death by fire and water was more widespread on the Continent and in North America, respectively), the Baglady's litany connects the four elements associated with a pre-Christian, earth-centred spirituality with the fate of the pre-Christian European tribes at the hands of hegemonic Christianity. The 'circularity' of pre-Christian reverence for the seasons, associated with the pagan figure of the god who dies and is reborn, collides, in the Baglady's monologue, with what Porter

Abbot has identified as the imperialist 'trope of onwardness',[8] which constructs a linear and binary cosmology through which the body of the countryside is 'cleansed' in the genocidal clearing away of the old religion and its supposed impurities. The historical subtext of the Baglady's monologue connects the early destruction of indigenous religious practices throughout Europe to the colonial destruction of Irish culture (embodied in the Baglady's connections to the conventional portrayal of colonized Ireland as a violated woman) and to the symbolically and sometimes literally violated position of women within the patriarchal family that was instituted in Ireland through colonial processes.

A further figuration of the persistence of the past into the present occurs in the river that the Baglady says 'is everywhere you look about you' (73) and in which she is destined to drown. In the monologue's water imagery, emotions are identified with history, both of which are ubiquitous. In her reading of the cards, the narrative and figurative collapse of emotions and history, of generational positioning, and of gender coalesce, pushing the audience toward an encounter with the monologue's elegized historical object: the lived truth of the Baglady's personal narrative, which has been brutally silenced.

Finally, the queen of hearts is transformed into the queen of spades, 'the quiet card'. The queen of spades has the face of a corpse: 'This woman has received a blow that will shut her up forever, but she's with you for all your life' (80-81). The last word of dialogue is the Baglady's ambiguous 'Drown.' Fintan O'Toole has written that *Baglady* 'reaches towards expiation,' reading this final word as addressed to the symbolic objects – the cards, the dress, the scarf, and the ring – of which she has divested herself.[9] I read these objects as pulling the Baglady down with them, although I agree that the scene, in its profound ambiguity, certainly reaches for expiation. The wedding ceremony that precedes the Baglady's final gesture – the dropping of the ring – formalizes an ongoing *Liebestod*, and her final gesture resonates with the import of Cleopatra's final words: 'Bridegroom, I come.'

In *Baglady*, we see the denial of history in the face of its contemporary persistence operating at its fatal worst. The connection that the play forges between the sacrificial colonial order and the loss of memory is figured in the Baglady, an amnesiac rape victim searching hopelessly for her slaughtered son. Mother Ireland, as she appears in the figure of the Baglady, is a fool who drowns in an ocean the nature of which she does not understand, pulled under by objects symbolizing Ireland's church-imposed gender relations.

The destruction of the Baglady by an internalized oppressor who began his work in the enforced silence of her childhood and finishes it off through an internalized system of remote control is reminiscent of the fate of actual incest survivors such as Virginia Woolf. As Louise DeSalvo has shown, Woolf was a survivor whose internalized identification with her childhood oppressor silenced her forever, finishing her off as she was writing the childhood memoirs in which she at last named her violators and admitted the significance of the past within her present consciousness.[10] The Baglady's death by immersion is also, however, a complex metaphor for the ways in which the colonial violation of national boundaries may produce its own disastrous and self-destructive silences. McGuinness illustrates the ways in which the maintenance of a suppressed and abject female subject position through the legal and political enforcement of the Oedipal family symbolizes but also literally perpetuates the colonized spaces out of which the deadly compulsion to silence and repeat the traumas of Ireland's historical past continually proceeds.

[1] Kumkum Sangari. 'The Politics of the Possible', *Cultural Critique* 7 (Fall 1987): 175.
[2] ibid.
[3] Fintan O'Toole. Interview with Frank McGuinness, *Sunday Tribune* (Dublin) 17 February 1985: 19.
[4] Frank McGuinness. *'Carthaginians' and 'Baglady.'* London: Faber and Faber, 1988. p.73. Subsequent references are to this edition.

5 She refers to the figure in her arms as 'them', suggesting both a specific withholding of gender and that the figure represents more than one person.
6 I am grateful to Elizabeth Cullingford for pointing out the resemblance between the Baglady, Our Lady of the Sorrows, and Kathleen ni Houlihan in her responses to an early draft of this chapter.
7 The 'court' cards (Queen, King, Page, Knight) signify woman and man, girl and boy of each element.
8 Porter Abbot. 'Preserving Beckett's Unfamiliarity.' Paper presented at the 1989 Yeats International Summer School, Sligo, Ireland, 18 August 1989.
9 Interview, *op cit.* p.19.
10 Louise De Salvo. *Virginia Woolf: The Impact of Childhood Sexual Abuse on her Life and Work.* NY:Ballantine Books, 1989.

The Masquerade of the Damned and the Deprivileging of Innocence: Frank McGuinness's *Innocence*.

Eamonn Jordan

> *All hatred driven hence, the soul recovers radical innocence.*[1]
> W.B. Yeats

For most people, the dilemmas of the creative artist seldom make great drama, and from a contemporary playwriting point of view, dramaturgical advice given to many aspiring playwrights would suggest that such considerations are a no-go area; in other words, avoid self-absorbed, articulate, pained, paranoid, self-reflective writers, actor-types, artists and, especially, poets at all costs.[2] From Pyper (failed sculptor) in *Observe the Sons of Ulster Marching Towards the Somme* (1985) and Dido (bad playwright and impostor, one of many characters with artistic leanings) in *Carthaginians* (1988), through Eleanor Henryson, the artist, in *The Bird Sanctuary* (1994), and the poets File, Edmund Spenser and poet/dramatist William Shakespeare in *Mutabilitie* (1997), and on to Gabriel and Conrad, characters of the theatre (loosely based on Micheál Mac Liammóir and Hilton Edwards respectively) in *Gates of Gold* (2002), McGuinness seems to take delight in rejecting any advice of the above kind, insisting that creative individuals and acts of imagination may be illuminating and brave, reactionary and conservative, but either way, there is the endeavour of work, a belief in the intensity of action, however the emphasis given to creativity may be interpreted, appreciated, rejected or despised.

When in 1986 McGuinness turned in *Innocence* to the great Italian post-Renaissance painter Michelangelo Merisi Caravaggio, the obvious question, even on a cursory level, is why?[3] (Why not a figure like Matt Talbot, whom Thomas Kilroy had so successfully utilized in *Talbot's Box* (1977) or Oscar and Constance Wilde as Kilroy had pursued in *The Secret Fall of Constance Wilde* (1997)? In effect, why not stay/play at home?) What really had the figure of Caravaggio to offer to an Irish playwright? What possible moral, political, cultural and historical parallels or symmetries might be available between a late twentieth-century Ireland and an Italy of the early 1600s? Is it too simple to think Italy and think Catholic, in the same way that many think of the Irish Republic as being predominantly consumed by Catholic issues? Looking at the play, one realizes very soon that something altogether more subtle is being expressed. On a broader scale, the deliberate use of Irish rather than Italian accents in the production of the play at the Gate Theatre is significant, as is the refusal to confine the play to any one historical period – an objective achieved by the use of anomalies and anachronisms in stage and costume designs, which ensured that the audience was forced to confront its own social and religious realities, through direct parallels with things that were becoming increasingly and actively highlighted by the media at that time, in terms of institutional violation and corruption by some members of religious orders.[4] The extent of such corruption has only now begun to take on a larger significance with the whole debate on paedophilia and the clerical abuse of power as I write in 2002: yet the implications for victims of such abuse are still not fully acknowledged or accepted. So while the play *Innocence* is of its time, its capacity to make visible what was somewhat hidden needs to be stressed in the here and now.

The scope of the play, the breadth of the focus, the dialogue between the two acts, the use of dramatic compression and the blending of fantasy, reality, dream and trauma in order to express something of Caravaggio's personal and artistic struggles and dilemmas, the complex melding of symbols and fragments from Caravaggio's paintings, as well as what the play does to the concept of subjectivity make it the great work that it is. In effect, the persona of Caravaggio and the backdrop of the social, religious and political order of the play fuse to create a dynamic chemistry.[5] There is no doubting the fact that outside of the Gate production of the play in 1986, directed by Patrick Mason, the vision and the blackness of the piece have been off-putting to many directors. Yet when one looks at the work of Sarah Kane, one finds strong parallels between her work and McGuinness's. I am not arguing that McGuinness wrote out of a similar darkness or bleakness, but that he has certain access, through his fictional character Caravaggio, to a type of vision typical of Kane. (From the outset it is obvious that one needs to distinguish between McGuinness's fictive character and the life of the artist Caravaggio – or versions of the life of the artist – something which many of the critics of Sebastian Barry's work *Hinterland* (2002) failed to do, all too easily and all too simplistically aligning Johnny Silvester with Charles J. Haughey.)[6]

Innocence is set on the day Caravaggio murders Ranuccio Tomassoni, but McGuinness's text shies well away from simplistic authenticity and from any type of documentary factuality, a death that is rumoured to have come about over a dispute during a court tennis match – court rage. McGuinness's Caravaggio is an angry protestor and subverter of norms, yet he is also a servant of the church, fretful about his allegiance to the institution and convinced of his own damnation, something that is brought about by the internalizing of church teaching on sexuality as much as anything else. The play is Catholic in its focus, but this is not to say that McGuinness was processing his own individual response to Catholicism, rather it is to argue that the piece, by necessity to be successful as a play, had to shift beyond the immediate concerns of the writer's own reflections and deliberations. To his credit, McGuinness does that and more. The work is anti-institutional, yet to say that the work is just anti-Catholic is to simplify it or de-mystify it. In this play the darkness of the painter is made obvious, as are his endeavours to articulate, to interpret, to sense and to see things not so much as they are, not as what they might be – in an aspirational sense – but from an eschewed, distraughtfully angular perspective. The painter is renowned for what is called a type of 'cellar raking light'. The paintings are noted for instances of intensity, or of near death moments or of death and the terror of the responses of those looking on, spaces where heaven and earth meet. There is a symbolic connection of the physical and metaphysical. Examples of these extremes would be in *The Sacrifice of Isaac*, a held or stalled instant at the moment of intended sacrifice, *The Crucifixion of St. Peter* with its near death moment or the after death moment in *The Deposition* or in *Judith Beheading Holofernes*, an instance of destruction, trauma and of pain. Other images of the moment of death occur in *The Death of the Virgin*, *The Crucifixion of St. Andrew*, *Salome with the Head of St. John the Baptist* and *David and Goliath*.

McGuinness's *The Factory Girls* (1982) stages the toil of a group of women against patriarchy and oppression and the struggle to articulate difference within socio-economic and imagistic/textual/narrative conventions (one needs narrative or complex images to envisage or to articulate protest), but as the drama progresses the characters become alert to their own innate conservatism as well, and in *Carthaginians*, the grief of the Derry community, post-Bloody Sunday (1972), is given substance and meaning through acknowledgment, but its intensity is deliberately destabilized through laughter, through the deep and soulful defiance of the fixed certainties that trauma can consolidate. As a consequence, hierarchies and meanings are contested, due in part to an intense liberation provoked and prompted by the framework play. Pain must be released and memory must be re-calibrated, before the joy or the dignity of living can be again realized.

In *Observe the Sons of Ulster Marching Towards the Somme* the soldiers realize that any notion of puerile, purifying sacrifice of the living, erupts not from some idealistic notion of the tribal or communal, but from an elemental blood lust, from deep self-hate and denial. The soldiers' shared version of masculinity is so corrupt from the outset that no self-evaluation can fully rectify it, but it can be altered — at least that is the hope. The soldiers settle for less, as they bleach the dry rhetoric of their language of its meaning, as they invert the convictions of courage and belonging that their tribal indoctrination encourages and as they shatter the rigid focus on destiny and inevitability. From such rupture something else is allowed entry, and from such a clash of perspectives an altogether different view of the world is given possible or potential credence. Potentiality arises from the corruption of certainty and from the violation of norms and expectations. In all of these plays there is a profound sense of disagreement, a profound sense of dissonance and disease, where darkness and light, failure and success misalign. Misalignment and the inability of meaning to be singular manage to corrupt the surface of the real. Laughter is often the alleviating grace, the ground upon which some sense of liberation is actioned. Intertextuality, ritual, lyricism, carnival, metatheatrical inversions, conscious and intuitive intertwining of forms trace out ambiguity and the limits of the real.

Although the work of Caravaggio provides intertextual and contextual springboards, *Innocence* is a play that questions beyond the frame through which the artist/writer imagines: one must ask *what* are the conventions and governing forms, *what* is representation, *what* are the implications of creative output, especially if the imagination is ideologically conditioned and if spectators' responses are culturally loaded? The Gate Theatre's audiences' responses, to the play's only Irish production, were very mixed, with some protesting at what they saw as sacrilegious. What are the limitations of art to vision or to initiate change or can art only tentatively hint at transformation through ironic juxtaposition and re-positioning? Across the whole body of McGuinness's theatre work there is a struggle to enunciate difference, without any single verifiable, immutable fact ever being articulated with deep conviction. Things shift and slide; any moral venture or approach is found suspect, any dignified or assertive posturing undermined, and any unconditional expression of certainty is suspect and inevitably combated and exposed as a weakness. Everything is threatened to such an extent that meaning while not endlessly or needlessly postponed is inevitably provisional, marginal, even liminal.

So why call this play *Innocence*? What does innocence mean? What is its polar opposite? In *Innocence*, we witness the corruption of the elect and the redemption of the damned. Then who are the conspirators; who are those that are complicit? What is power; what is abuse and what is the abuse of power? What is violation? What is corruption? How active or passive might an individual be in the sanctioning of abuse? For some, innocence is a camouflage, behind which the first world liberal capitalist order establishes control and denies complicity. Elsewhere, I have suggested 'Innocence destroyed by non-consensual violation has been a frequent recurrence in today's Irish theatrical practices, an innocence that is neither holy nor foolish', so that 'stock innocence or foregrounded innocence as a construct, must be destabilized, because its constitution in the main is passive and not active; innocence in this form is never 'other'. Innocence can contribute to a state of symbolic disorder through the frame of absence, delivered by the figure of the dead child. The absence/presence dichotomy is made problematic'.[7] There are irreconcilable differences between salvation and innocence. It may well be that innocence is no longer sacred, but a superstition. Yet Mikami claims that 'It seems that McGuinness holds the view that to be an artist one must also possess a kind of deep innocence at one's core',[8] and she argues also for the notion of 'innocence at creativity's core'.[9] That probably is too positive an appreciation. McGuinness of course can be seen as the source of that prompting. Of Caravaggio's work, McGuinness states that what lingers is 'some wonderful power that is innocent and strong'.[10] But the detail of the play doesn't testify completely to that.[11] In many respects McGuinness can be considered the major player in the articulation of the idea of innocence, one that is fundamentally positioned within a post-colonial consciousness, one that is fundamentally driven by a quest for rest, one that can give validation and provisional meaning. Innocence is often seen as a stable and insatiable configuration, where a notional uncorrupted defiance may lay hold. (It is evident across most of McGuinness's plays;

his soldiers in *Observe the Sons of Ulster* believed that their battle was between the elect and the damned.) Raymond Williams' oft used idea of a 'structure of feeling' can be re-configured here as a structure of innocence. It is a structure of thought, an insistence on something that crops up in this play in a variety of guises, initially in the form of binary oppositions – disease and cleanliness, good and evil, and damnation and salvation. Any hierarchial arrangement between innocence and damnation is contested. There is a certain dispossession of innocence. In such a way, the play politicizes the concept of innocence.

The Catholic religion has institutionalized innocence in the form of the Virgin Mary, a person uncorrupted, pure, unsullied, unmarked in a way by human frailty or sin. Sins corrupt. Sin can also damn. Children have always been associated, biblically speaking, with innocence (the slaughter of the innocent), yet the ramifications of such violation become profoundly blatant in this play. Within that grid, McGuinness exploits the role of art in society, the rage, compassion, dismissal, savagery, tenderness of the individual artist, the practice of patronage in various guises, the controlling brutality of some religious figures, the exploitation, both economic and sexual, of the poor, the function of articulation. (While Lucio and Antonio, the 'Rough Trade', are not children, their dependence on selling their bodies for material sustenance must be noted.) Through these things McGuinness somehow challenges the conventions of a society that at that time of the play's first production in Ireland, outlawed homosexuality, queries the indulgences of wealth, the capacity of an individual to buy and sell, to be bought and sold, considers what is omission and commission, neglect and abuse, and also challenges the violence implicit in constitutional conservatism, social discrimination (gay bashing and here noticeably its converse), and just as importantly the centrality of violence both to history and to Irish history in particular. During the First Act Caravaggio's brother urges him to come home and 'live clean', telling Caravaggio that all there is for him in Rome is 'disease and dirt' (*I* 250). Caravaggio states that he does not 'know where to find it [home]' but he does know that it is not where he was born (*I* 251). So innocence has no association with the sanctuary of home, where things can be grounded, where elemental values can be espoused with depth, intensity or complete validation. Home proves to be no site of ultimate verification or authenticity, but one of rupture. Here the idea of innocence cannot be without guile. Normally when we see innocence in films, the characters display some disabilities, mental or physical. Caravaggio is no Forrest Gump. There is no innocent pre-Edenic reality in *Innocence*. In the McGuinness drama innocence and damnation are propositioned as polar opposite positions, only to be eschewed, within the interconnected frameworks of sexuality, creativity and violence. The first part of the play is called 'life' the second 'death', but in 'life' death is found and in 'death' life is found, so in damnation innocence can prosper, in ugliness beauty can reign.

This is not a play about art alone, this is not a play only about the creativity and destruction of the artist, and this is not a play just about institutional violation. It is a play about how individual agency can be articulated and achieved and how the concept of innocence proves to be some structure of meaning through which these things can be interrogated? It is easy to accept that power abuses, but does art also abuse, and, if so, in what ways? What is violation within the framework of representation and what does the artist Caravaggio or his work offer to McGuinness by way of difference, articulation, resistance and vision in order to comment on contemporary society? Just as importantly, how is that placed in dramatic form?

In a way, Pyper's failure in *Observe the Sons of Ulster* to carve, to articulate, to accept his silencing as a communicator of vision is replaced by the almost heretical, impetuosity of Caravaggio's artistry in *Innocence*. Caravaggio, unlike Pyper, does not survive by the play's end, yet the artistry of the painter has lived on down the ages, revealing as much about the circumstances of his own society as the condition and the state of his own mind as he worked, something that is viewed of course through our own contemporary templates of interpretation. When it comes to laughter in *Innocence*, something altogether different occurs, for in almost all of McGuinness's other plays, none has the darkness, none has the relentlessness of focus and none has the deep sense of corruption that is built on frailty, rage and sheer destruction. Caravaggio feels himself to be damned, even if he mockingly can tell Lucio and Antonio that he is 'a saint' (*I* 230).

Regardless, he can envision beauty and salvation in the guise of others, who are rejected, labelled and cast aside by society and who live on the fringes in squalor and with little dignity. The play takes its inspiration from Caravaggio's central placing of the socially dispossessed in his paintings/stagings. He used beggars, vagabonds, prostitutes and thieves, even the dead as models. If Christian doctrine is to be believed, these are the ones that will receive heavenly salvation, and they are the ones that receive the provisional salvation of the artist, who transposes them from one reality to another, who moulds the negative into something positive. Is poverty an intolerable price to pay for salvation? The bigger question is this I suppose. So there is an obviously huge political agenda, both explicit and implicit, in the paintings of Caravaggio. In his own time people rejected his humanizing of the saints – clued in, unconsciously perhaps, to some deeper transgression. By using the lowly, Caravaggio was in fact painting their potential salvation, yet the church perhaps only gave lip service to that reality in the way that it treated those who were in poor circumstances. The Cardinal indulged in excess, unwilling to share his food and his surplus with others. No miracle of the loaves here, no reflection on lost opportunity. Instead poverty was acceptable, through irresponsibility and the absence of brotherhood or sisterhood. This is not to deny the charity of the church down through the ages.

In order to represent the vision and in order to make the images or paintings of Caravaggio's work realizable, McGuinness resorts to a specific type of staging, particularly in the creation of the opening and closing stage images and more importantly as ways of theatricalizing the spiritual and socio/economic reality of the world of Caravaggio by connecting up light and dark, vision and destruction, salvation and damnation, all of which is ultimately prompted by the consciousness of the living dead. In the programme note to the play, speaking of Caravaggio and Lena, McGuinness states that 'the woman he honoured must have been a match for him, and being Caravaggio, it must have been a queer match. So I began to paint, to play'.[12] The linking of painting and play is vital.

The play, at first sight, appears to work within a dialectical model, with act one and act two, life and death, predominantly reality and dream, relating to each other or as flip sides of each other. Such neatness collapses on closer inspection, as such distinctions are run into the ground, through inversion and licence, through perverse juxtaposition and through a deeply unsettlingly reflection on living. The opening tableau of the play shows Caravaggio, sleeping in Lena's hovel, experiencing a nightmare. It is a collaged event, including the characters of the Cardinal, Lena, and Caravaggio's sister and brother and involves the assembling of some not so random fragments from the paintings of Caravaggio. Specific objects like a skull, a red cloak and the horse emerge, and these recur with some regularity across the work of the Italian painter.

Worth pursuing just a little are the mobile and the transformative qualities of the cloak for instance. In the first moments of the play the cloak is used to symbolize a horse, then it adjusts when Lena caresses it as if it were a child. When the dream sequence ends and we are back in the real world Lena examines the garment, noticing that it is in need of repair. She calls it flippantly the 'same old ball-covering' (I 206). At the end of the first act Antonio removes the cloak from the Cardinal's premises. Towards the end of the play, Lena, taking it from the bag of booty, lays claim to it. Soon after, Lena places it around Antonio's body in a re-construction of Caravaggio's painting of *St. John the Baptist*. Such repeated prominence releases an elaborate irony – given that such a cloak had been used to such intertexual effect in many of Caravaggio's greatest paintings themselves.[13] The beauty of the cloak in the paintings reverberates against the tattered nature of the cloak in reality – its symbolic value resonates side by side with the innate functionality and daily usage of the object. Moreover, this visual and sensual melding of these two realities, that of the lived life and the work of art suggests not only the inter-relatedness between the life and the art and of course the drives and motivations behind the work of art, but also calls attention to the feigned, grotesque theatricality of Caravaggio's later paintings.[14] So a subversive structure of intent can be extrapolated from the use of props in this play even from this early stage.

The painter in an early conversation with Lena sets down the view of his own work: 'In all of Rome I stand supremely alone as painter, seer and visionary, great interpreter of man' (*I* 208), and again, 'For my art balances the beautiful and the ugly, the saved and the sinning' (*I* 208). By taking 'ordinary flesh and blood and bone' with his hands he can transform it 'into eternal light, eternal dark', because Caravaggio believes that he paints as 'God intended the eyes to see and to see is to be God' (*I* 208). Regardless of the difficulties and substantially prompted by Caravaggio's subversions of the patronage structure, McGuinness manages his own type of subversive dramaturgy. Early on in the play we discover that Lena has previously modelled for Caravaggio. 'Caravaggio: I gathered the earth's fruit and the tree's leaf and I plant them in your face for your face is a bowl full of life, full of Lena' (*I* 218). Lena's face, McGuinness hints, was the inspiration for Caravaggio's paintings either in *The Boy with the Bowl of Fruit*, the still life *The Bowl of Fruit* or the bowl of fruit in the later painting, *The Supper at Emmaus*. Her face serves as inspiration, yet the licence of the inspiration is to detail death and decay. The ordinary is transformed into the eternal and the damned, but from the earliest stages of the play, we know not to take Caravaggio too seriously. We can see this trajectory happening early on, when having commented on the beauty of Lena's face as detailed above, he goes on to blow his nose into his hands (*I* 218).

The Whore (Anna), Antonio and Lucio also modelled for Caravaggio. What has he done to them or for them? The Whore, it is suggested, appears in *Death of the Virgin*. (An often claimed, but unproven fact is that Caravaggio painted *The Death of the Virgin* using the dead and bloated body of a prostitute who had drowned herself in a river.[15]) Antonio, it is suggested, is portrayed as the character in *The Boy with the Bowl of Fruit*. Lucio recalls how Caravaggio dressed him up as a tree – as homo-eroticized subject/object – squeezing grapes all over him and calling him Bacchus (*I* 225).[16] The relationship between Caravaggio and Lena opens up the specific issues of homosexuality from the start. As Lena roughly masturbates Caravaggio early on in the play 'the hand of God' is given an altogether new meaning (*I* 210). Later, after that, both self-consciously perform in a mock-romantic scenario, where it is feigned that Caravaggio has proposed marriage. (The Whore goes so far as to call Lena and Caravaggio the 'holy family' [*I* 215].) And although both Caravaggio and Lena indulge in parodic games of mock heterosexual love, their discussion of a dead child seems to suggest somehow, although it is less likely, that Caravaggio may have been bisexual. Regardless, its symbolic significance cannot be ignored. There are attempts by many of the characters in the play to make strong associations with the darkness and Caravaggio's sexuality. While there is a strong sense that Caravaggio's inability to accept his sexuality leads to dysfunctionality on a certain level, I think the darkness has as much if not more to do with the Jungian concept of shadow. Innocence is corruption's shadow and vice versa.[17] Because Caravaggio is homosexual, the sexual transgression in the play is doubly violatory, given homosexuality was illegal in Ireland at the time of the play's first performance and most certainly disapproved of by the Catholic Church at the time of the painter's existence. To have such subtle, outrageous and sophisticated subversions taking place is of substantial interest.

The very darkness of Caravaggio's art has been spoken of by McGuinness when discussing Caravaggio's triptych, *The Calling of St. Matthew* (also known as *St. Matthew and the Angel*), *The Martyrdom of St. Matthew*, *The Inspiration of Saint Matthew* at the Contarelli Chapel, San Luigi dei Francesi, Rome. McGuinness claims that if one is to:

> Stand long enough looking at it in darkness and the strength and the order of its events, even its power of colour, start to make their force felt, even in the negative. Both inside the painting and inside yourself ... something is happening, black and frightening and of great violence. Christ knows what conditions Caravaggio has established, but they're there, and then you can either panic or dance in the dark, for the ob-

> server is within the control of a great artist, who has painted his triptych and told his story simultaneously and subversively.[18]

The connection made by McGuinness between the 'darkness', 'violence' and a threatening clarity is pointed. Accounts of the painter's life hint at the consistency of violence:

> In 1600 he was accused of blows by a fellow painter, and the following year he wounded a soldier. In 1603 he was imprisoned on the complaint of another painter and released only through the intercession of the French ambassador. In April 1604 he was accused of throwing a plate of artichokes in the face of a waiter, and in October he was arrested for throwing stones at the Roman Guards. In May 1605 he was seized for misuse of arms, and on July 29 he had to flee Rome for a time because he had wounded a man in defense of his mistress. Within a year, on May 29, 1606, again in Rome, during a furious brawl over a disputed score in a game of tennis, Caravaggio killed one Ranuccio Tomassoni.[19]

Art takes place in a context and here the context of Catholic doctrine and patronage, in particular, are considered. The Cardinal's pre-eminence in the lived world is obvious, buying what he wishes – art and people. Patronage is presented without any benefactorial sentiment. The artist is a chattel, but in the instance of Caravaggio something also to be feared. His waywardness needs discipline, and while he is submissive, Caravaggio still will not accept fully the codes of silence and respect. As Caravaggio states he is '... painter and pimp. Painter to Cardinal del Monte, pimp to the Papal Curia, whore to the catholic church' (*I* 239). (It is reputed that Caravaggio painted about forty works under the Cardinal's patronage.)

As an artist, Caravaggio has little choice but to embrace the patronage of the church. As a dependent on such a structure, he also functions as a pimp for the cardinal. If you interconnect the two things, what emerges? Is the concept of patronage totally akin to an act of prostitution, or is that too simplistic? Does poverty dictate the actions of the poor who turn primarily to prostitution? Can morality be brought to bear on it? Does hunger move people outside the frame of morality? While the sexuality of the two male prostitutes is somewhat confused, their anger in having to sell their bodies is also made apparent to an audience. Caravaggio provides the Cardinal with the two young men as a 'gift' (*I* 237), but it is anything but a gift. The capacity to buy lives, to purchase sex, to turn or transubstantiate humans to objects, is the ultimate expression of power. The Cardinal wonders if Caravaggio has begun to enjoy 'playing' his 'fool'(*I* 242)? Caravaggio resists that suggestion, instead reminding his patron that it is his blessing that he yearns for and this is why he is a willing participant in his own subjugation (*I* 242). 'Cardinal: ... You believe with a depth that is frightening. And with a vision that is divine' (*I* 242-3). Can we state unequivocally that playing is not only about contesting subjugation, but a way of postponing hierarchy and a way of complicating relationships? Is playing a way of lessening the impact of power, a poor person's strategy to place a false perception of enablement in the mind of the vulnerable?

The first act ends with two acts of destruction, deeds that articulate the hostility towards the Cardinal's exploitation: Caravaggio destroys the paintings and tapestries on the walls and Antonio and Lucio steal a bag of booty from the Cardinal's palace. (Ransacking is a key concept that had already appeared in *Observe the Sons of Ulster*: 'The temple of the Lord is darkness. He has ransacked his dwelling' (*Obs* 100).) The desecration of the Cardinal's dwelling leads on to the death of the man that Caravaggio kills. Caravaggio returns home to Lena's hovel bloodied from the fight. Lucio simplifies the tension of the fight, clearly romanticizing it (*I* 262). In that way, the violence has come full circle. The violence and intensity of the artistic vision could only find release in murder. Caravaggio equates death and beauty, death and touch (indirect hint at the issue of AIDS): 'Finally, we touched' (*I* 265).[20] The terrifying world of reality is displaced during the second act by the nightmare world of the dream. Early in the play Caravaggio exclaims that 'all life is death, all light is darkness' (*I* 238). Here the artist must stare down the ghosts which haunt him (like Pyper in *Observe the Sons of Ulster*, but Caravaggio's ghosts are more interactive) and through the dream/nightmare Caravaggio finds some solace, but never enough to grant an absolution. Caterina is the first figure to appear during the dream sequence. When Caravaggio meets her, he thinks that he is in the grave. Instead he is in a dream – from grave to dream, from dream to grave. Caterina tells of her death during childbirth and how she was sacrificed to save the life of her son. Her rage is against the world. She is sacrificed to ensure the survival of her son.

The figures that haunt him must find release and give freedom as well. Caravaggio endeavours to free his models (who earlier saw themselves in part as 'victims' of the painter [*I* 278]), as the models emancipate Caravaggio. In the real world of the play, excess and starvation co-exist. The paintings offer temporary release, fantastic imaginings of difference. But no absolutions are offered by these temporary, almost carnivalized aberrations. Despite these subversions, disease, drowning and starvation were the lot of the models. Caravaggio's response to such fatalities is of great interest. As he has no solution to their problems, he thus cannot be culpable? Or can he? For it is only in the dreamscape that Caravaggio can offer the possibility of change, when he wipes the models clean. If there is some notion of release to be found in the reversals and dynamic subversions of the work, there are also other types of subversions with their own distinctive ramifications, as previously argued.

In effect, McGuinness brings the play within a dream consciousness in order to deliver a state of reversibility, proliferation and licence, where the main subversive force is taken from the rejection of negativity and by the preparation of a space for creativity and living, all of which takes place within a structure where life and death co-mingle and the terrors of both are reconciled. To do so, he builds on the reversal of the hierarchical dynamics of the real world, and he accesses a spirit of play through the spirit of the animal world. Through both, innocence becomes the focal point. In the dream, Caravaggio dries the flesh of The Whore, who had drowned, cleanses the face of Antonio and he kisses life back into Lucio. Having done so, he invites his dream figures (aspects of himself, perhaps) to play. There is an exchange of performative, transactional healing that builds on the concept of animal play introduced in the first act. Caravaggio can awaken from the death of dream or the grave of the dream and back to the living. Life not death has the pulling power.

Through the deployment of animal imagery, McGuinness broadens the perspective of meaning and violence within the play. Animal imagery often represents the deepest representation of repression and transference. The inhabiting of the animal space is often a way of getting in touch with more elemental forces, archetypal energies that can hint at immobility or its counter-force and thus formulate change. Likewise an audience member may consider the question or the particular use of animal imagery in the paintings of Caravaggio. Various types of animals appear regularly in the paintings – a lizard is present in *The Boy Bitten by Lizard*, one of the pictures of *St. John the Baptist* includes a ram, and *The Conversion of St. Paul* has a white horse. The animals in the paintings earth the artist's vision along with calling attention to sensuous and sexual energies, which the Catholic religion finds almost impossible to accept as healthy, even within marriage.

In the play itself a horse appears in the opening dream sequence and later on Caravaggio claims that a horse had kicked him, almost blinding him. (Lucio states that Caravaggio has a face like 'a horse's arse' [*I* 224].) But the horse is also a symbol of power and oppression, and its association with blindness links the horse with the fear of castration. (See Peter Shaffer's play *Equus* [1973] for its use of symbolism and McGuinness's *The Factory Girls* for the emphasis on the story of the girl in the comic *Bunty* who escapes on a horse and *Observe the Sons of Ulster* for the mock battle of the Boyne/Scarva and the horse play therein.) It is no coincidence that after the nightmare, which opens the first act, Caravaggio is suffering from an eye complaint. Lucio was also wounded by a horse and Antonio by a rat (*I* 234). The characters have wounds inflicted by animals. Wounded by animals, overcoming the animal, energized by the elemental energy of the animal, becoming the animal, all seem to be part of the process that McGuinness suggests. Early in the play the Cardinal likens Caravaggio to an animal – as the fawning Caravaggio moves about on all fours before the Cardinal, something that serves both as a gesture of submissiveness and as an expression of his base self. **Cardinal:** Don't fear my animal either' (*I*: 240), a statement that suggests that within the carnivalized frame, all is not possible. Here we are within the terrain of animal instincts, an instinctive force that is predatorial, cruel and violent.

During the first act, in the Cardinal's room Lucio and Antonio 'mock-fight about the room' (*I* 232). It is a sort of carnival of the animals. 'Lucio bays like a hound', Antonio becomes a hare at Caravaggio's suggestion, Lucio changes into a 'wild horse' who attacks Antonio and then is transformed into a 'trusty steed' (again echoes of *Observe the Sons of Ulster*) after Caravaggio 'touches' his face (*I* 233). It is significant that Lucio rejects the role, instead preferring to be a 'dragon', thereby establishing his own sense of autonomy. Antonio is given the gift of flight, and he turns into 'a fighting bird. An eagle' (*I* 233). Taken in by the licence of metamorphosis, next Lucio transforms into a bull. They fight, on equal footing. Caravaggio becomes a 'poisonous lizard' (*I* 233). Eventually the two men become 'unicorns' (*I* 233), mystical animals that Caravaggio and Lena had played at a little earlier. Antonio remarks that 'that was great', as expressive of the joy garnered from the possibilities of transformation (*I* 233). (Poison, touching and kissing become indelibly linked. Touch brings transformation, touch brings death, as touch is how Caravaggio describes the act of murder, as previously mentioned.) The impetus to transform comes from Lucio, who early in the play calls his clients 'animals' (*I* 229), and now, in the carnival scene, he would like to slice 'the wrinkled old shits to ribbons' with 'his nails' (*I* 232). The game begins with Lucio imitating 'an animal clawing' (*I* 232). Play, rage and revenge coalesce. Building on this transaction, during the second act when Caravaggio dreams, his Sister invokes the names of animals and invites further transgressions. Within the world of the dream the nature of the transformations gains added purpose, as they relinquish the confinements of the real.

> **Sister:** Who is the bird whose song is golden?
> Dragon, breathe your web of fire.
> Steed, open your trusty mouth.
> Bull, charge with a beating heart.
> Lizard, change colour for ever.
> Hare, lie with sleeping lion.
> Eagle, see with all-seeing eye.
> Hound, play with the wounded lion.
> Who is the bird whose song is golden?
> Unicorn, preserve the species.
> Unicorn, protect the species.
> Unicorn, preserve the species.
> Unicorn, protect the species (I 280).[21]

The goal of this message of transgression is to 'live'. In the dream sequence, the Cardinal appears in rags, as the Cardinal and his servant have reversed places: 'The servant opens his shirt and the Cardinal goes to suck his breasts. Servant hurls him away' (I 274). There is a complete reversal of power. Also, the Cardinal performs a mock benediction: 'Blessed be the hands that anoint me with iron. Blessed be the tongue that spits curses on my head. Blessed be the feet that walk the way of damnation' (I, 275). In a similar vein, and earlier on in the play, McGuinness allows Lucio and Antonio perform a mock ceremony of transubstantiation, something that surely disturbs the reverence usually paid to the ritualistic religious act.

> **Lucio:** This is my body.
> **Antonio:** This is my blood.
> **Lucio:** Turn me into bread, God.
> **Antonio:** Me into wine.
> **Lucio:** Give us a miracle.
> **Antonio:** Give us a man (I 222).

The body of Christ adjusts and takes the shape of the carnivalized body, what Lucio calls 'a reverse job. Flesh and blood into bread and wine' (I 222). Haunted by the ghosts of his family and his models, Caravaggio promises to bring 'peace to what' he paints' (I 279). This is the gesture of reconciliation and the gesture of compassionate healing through transformation. With the precepts of carnival, a baser world is enunciated, where the body, reversed social hierarchies and the absence of God are validated. Substantially, fear and failure are mocked and not only is deviance tolerated, but it is accepted, treated as the norm. Carnival dismisses the ideas of transcendence and dispenses with a narrow concept of beauty. In the paintings, not only does Caravaggio humanize the saints painted, he also captures an earthiness, a heaviness, rather than any ethereal essence. In Caravaggio's work there is no idealization of saints. Previously, saintly figures were portrayed with eyes towards heaven only, seldom towards the things of the world. The corruption of the material world was the burden. Caravaggio painted the saints and grounded them in this material reality, a reality that must be recognized and fought over. So McGuinness by inverting ritual, by ensuring the secularization of religious ritual and by disconcerting language from its rational transparency through carnival, ensures that images of order are subverted from within. As such, carnival and reconciliation are co-joined. How can a church that promises salvation, use the work of the damned to illustrate the potential of salvation and its possibility? How can it be that it is only the damned who can mock salvation and justice and who can bring some sense of transformation? Perversely, damnation is the only thing offering redemption. '**Caravaggio:** I curse my life. I damn my soul. Trust me' (*I* 255).

Even after the nightmare, Caravaggio cannot fully face life and light, as he still calls on his father to tell him a 'story', as Edward does in *Someone Who'll Watch Over Me* (1992). His very strong fear of the dark is made obvious, yet his paintings articulate that very same darkness with intensity and conviction. (Caravaggio, had earlier, begged his brother not to leave him in the dark [*I* 254]). The play ends with the physical absence of Caravaggio, but his spirit survives through his paintings. In the final sequence of the play Lena dreams that she stood in a beautiful room with Caravaggio's pictures on the walls and that the painter had found peace. Lena laughs because she realizes that Caravaggio was looking down from above, having found salvation in heaven. 'Lena: I knew then somehow we'd won, we turned the world upside down, the goat and The Whore, the queer and his woman' (*I* 284).²² But McGuinness could not exit only with such optimism, so he affords Lena the opportunity to add that 'the virgin of the forest is a cheap whore and the unicorn's a stupid goat... this whore's a tired woman and my goat is a broken unicorn' (*I* 284).²³ And in order to articulate and to emphasize the appropriations that the production of the play also took, Lena is enabled. She takes the chalice, cross, bowl and cloak from the bag of church booty, and both secularizes and re-distributes its images and symbols. Lena demands that Antonio strip naked so that he can pose for her interpretation of Caravaggio's painting *John the Baptist*. The cycle is complete; the gift is passed on, and an audience may be empowered likewise? During the opening minutes of the play Caravaggio arrogantly and repetitively lists his name and his talents, promising to keep it up until he is poured a drink. Caravaggio plays the role of visionary and pompous artist in an effort to antagonize Lena. But more importantly, this playfulness becomes something altogether different when she plays the role of artist by the end of the play, whereby a different scale of enablement is revealed. His self-perception exposes aspiration and playfulness at the same time, a knowingness about his own talent and a self-depreciating streak that keeps arrogance in check. Moreover the significance of play during these scenes helps to raise some of the more serious issues in a more casual manner. Play moves characters from object to subject, and back again: characters are on some quest for a subjective position, but the notion of a de-centred, scattered self is more obvious than one which is consistent and coherent. Self-objectification, self-deconstruction, self-codification of the individual becomes obvious. Thus subjectivity is stretched across a continuum. (Caravaggio: ... I am my brother. I am my sister (*I* 253).) The fluidity of space, matches the fluidity of self, the multiplicity of selves and tendency of Caravaggio to use the same models across a range of paintings highlights his subversive intent and also the concept of proliferation. (The sister plays the additional roles of Caravaggio's father and mother.) Here, the visionary, aspirational beauty of the artist springs from the same individual that can brutally murder; the artist that can deploy his brush to generate elegance is the same one that can shape death with a knife.

McGuinness draws upon Athol Fugard's *Dimetos*, which takes its inspiration from an extract from Albert Camus's notebooks.[24] In Fugard's play, a retired Engineer attempts to occlude himself from any responsibility for the nature and structure of his own society. Dimetos's adopted niece commits suicide as a despairing response to the fact that he, Dimetos, watched as a man tried to rape her. Fugard's play considers creativity, community and intervention. It is the darkness of the vision found in the play that inspires McGuinness. Dimetos naively thought 'innocence was still possible' (*Dimetos* 39). A decaying carcass that washes up onto the shore beside Dimetos's house has a stench emanating from it. The smell increases to such an extent that it drives Dimetos mad. The parental role given to Dimetos is abused and as a consequence the niece cannot cope with his negligence, his complicity and his absence of innocence.

In *Innocence*, Caravaggio's brother urges the painter to father a child, as if a child would not only extend the family line, but also place Caravaggio differently in the world. During the final exchange between Caravaggio and Lena, he shifts the conversation from her emphasis 'The dead' to 'Our Dead' (*I* 268). At that point, 'Lena starts to cradle an imaginary child'. There is a suggestion of miscarriage. The conversation is devoid of the playfulness that seemed to have mocked romantic heterosexual love. 'Lena: Never look at me again. Never touch me.' The connection between life and death is complete. Sex and touch: sex and death. The symbol's significance is broadened further by the fact that Caravaggio could not 'give' her 'a birth', for Caravaggio, according to her, only brings 'death' (*I* 269). The impossibility of giving new life is superimposed upon Caravaggio's murderous activity, the taking of life. He is equated temporarily with darkness. Sexuality, absence of birth and death are interlinked. Her dismissal of him is as follows: 'See the queer. See his darkness. See yourself. Don't see me. Don't see me any more' (*I* 269). (The reason why Caravaggio murdered the man has partly got to do with the fact that he had called them 'girls' according to Lucio [*I* 262].) Male homosexuality is directly associated with absence and with the physical impossibility of procreating children and during the first act, in some senses, homosexuality is equated with homelessness, to be without sanctuary or repose. But McGuinness is careful to progress to a point where Caravaggio is more accepting, less guilty and less apologetic about his sexuality. Caravaggio's brother rejects him first of all because Caravaggio cannot prolong the family name and secondly because Caravaggio would be a danger to children (*I* 248). ('Caravaggio: They eat their young in Naples' [*I* 267].) The radical act of abuse against children is seen as the way of shattering innocence, something that the general public radically miscalculates by associating occasionally homosexuality with paedophilia. Abuse is made central in a way. Artistry and giving birth are interconnected. It is as if the work of the artist compensates for the absence of a child, or like in Ibsen's *Hedda Gabler*, Lovborg's manuscript is the symbolic equivalent to a child. Neither a child nor a work of art offers the potential of innocence. Apart from the imaginary child, the other child in the play becomes something altogether different. Childbirth led to the death of Caterina. 'Sister: The child poisoned me' (*I* 271). 'Sister: I cursed all children and all fathers and I cursed God for creating woman' (*I* 271-2). In such a manner, McGuinness is clearly contesting the association of the child with innocence and the possibility that occurs with it happens in so many plays. (See Thomas Murphy's *Bailegangaire* (1985) as the great example.) As I have argued elsewhere when or if 'a regurgitated, sentimentalized and sometimes eroticized innocence of the child becomes used as a marker against the tribulations of the adult world or as an emblem of possibility, as if only it can be free of the taint of compromise, then we are entering a period of crisis, dramaturgically speaking'.[25] Instead a different type of calibrated innocence is proposed in this play.

Innocence plays with the nature of art, conventions and symbols of Catholicism, deconstructing or inverting associated meaning, indirectly breaching the conventions and assumptions of a belief system of religion, and of a society that divides rich and poor. It is just as simplistic to argue that the painter exploited his models, as it is to place a value on the act of ritual cleansing in the dream sequence – and that by drying The Whore's face, wiping the disease from Antonio's face and kissing Lucio, is a way of alleviating responsibility? Dramatically, if nothing else, it is astute. Moreover it is the incapacity of the artist to have a deep impact on social structures, as he/she is both complicit and dependent. More tellingly the inability to evade the material reality is of much more interesting substance. Neither is it a justification of the artist to remain outside the frame of responsibility nor is it a justification for inaction. Apart from the opening and closing tableau, through the layering of the first and second acts, through the interplay between these acts, indeed the co-dependency of both acts, life and dream, reality and dream, between the substantially public landscape of the first act and private, mainly introverted, landscape of the second act, an unique type of configuration is made available to an audience. Moreover the ability of the playwright to invert light and dark, good and evil, beauty and the ugly, buyer and bought, rich and poor has serious implications.

In this play the central tensions between creativity and destruction, expression and chaos, damnation and salvation, death and life, and body and soul hit home in the most outrageous and frightening manner. In a world of power, authority and violation, not to mention poverty and prostitution, is innocence an unratifiable quantity and is innocence the greatest stroke that ideology and religion can pull? Lena states 'I was mad about Our Lady when I was a girl. Christ, would you believe that? I used to imagine I was her daughter and Jesus was a right pup who tormented me. The innocence of it' (*I* 209). In addition, The Whore (Anna) ironically narrates a vision of Jesus Christ who honours her by giving her a message (*I* 257-8). Anna's message during her vision is that the Pope is without sin; that he is a saint, but the corruption of the church is from the top down, given the cardinal's remorseless exploitation of the needy.

Instead of goodness and virtue, we get corruption, hidden behind the veil of innocence. In the 1980s the Catholic Church in Ireland began to face down lots of criticism, its inability to deal with the complexity of the contemporary living, its negative attitudes towards homosexuality and its refusal to face up to the issue of clerical sexual abuse, and its complicity in covering up scandals. (Caravaggio tells his brother that he has 'been up the arses of more priests', and this would strike home even closer in a modern production of this play. It is not that sexuality is a problem, but it is the hypocrisy and the pretence of celibacy to which many take offence.) Within the frame of the play the Church through its patronage also exploits the artist, who needs the commissions to survive. Moreover, the ability of the church to damn becomes the strongest force in the shaping of Caravaggio's consciousness. Sin brings the destruction of innocence: sin brings damnation. The capacity of the powerful to name, accuse, implicate and to damn is questioned and the intentions behind such gestures are exposed. It is within this context that we must judge Caravaggio. The Models claim that not only did Caravaggio use them to gain his own success and they were his victims, but that they also form part of his reputation, as they were his inspiration. They want both recognition and compensation. And his response: 'Caravaggio: I fashioned you into a golden bowl and whoever eats from you will be clean for you are without blemish' (I 279). By 'without blemish', does McGuinness mean innocent? What is the justification for this type of airbrushing: is it only for the sake of beauty or how can we unravel the subversive intent? Is reparation only possible on an imaginary level?

When Lucio and Antonio are with the Cardinal, Caravaggio pounces on Antonio and holds a knife to his throat. Caravaggio asks, 'Has the big, bad wolf put the fear of God into your innocent souls (I 241)? Here the Cardinal sees things in animal terms; Caravaggio is the wolf, the two male prostitutes are called mockingly perhaps 'innocent souls', but the fluidity and the multiple meanings of the terms 'innocent' and 'animals' becomes increasingly apparent.[26] Earlier in the play the Cardinal had called Lucio and Antonio 'poor lambs' (I 241). Biblically speaking, lambs were associated with innocence. On one level they are innocent, yet on another they have no access to innocence, given the degree of corruption that surrounds them, given their participation in the corruption and exploitation, yet the economic reality of their existence ensures that they cannot rely on any value system that confirms innocence. Corruption and compromise are the order of the day. Caravaggio pleads to his models that he is 'innocent of all' they throw at him. (*I* 277) The artist expresses that even the wildest animal is 'innocent at heart', but, although Caravaggio has a 'way with animals', the human may be animal by way of instinct, but ultimately cannot be animal by way of reason (*I* 235). As previously argued, innocence is increasingly the fault-line in contemporary Irish theatre, innocence cannot be the prerequisite of identity. Instead it is a phantom space. What would be the disorienting impact if carnage and destruction were considered to be at the core of being, so that neither salvation nor damnation retains their unbending opposition? (In *Carthaginians* those that died on Bloody Sunday can have the tag of innocence. 'The innocent dead. There's thirteen dead in Derry' (*C* 352).)

With life comes responsibility, and innocence is but a difficult part of that. The quest for innocence is made problematic within the frame of this play, for neither a naturalized, pastoralized innocence nor a redeemable religious innocence are accessible. Innocence cannot embrace the compromises, violence, rage, destructiveness, vengeance and pettiness of living, without losing its fortitude. *Innocence* marks not so much innocence destroyed as innocence as a site incapable of significant demarcations. In addition, the abuse of privilege in the play also serves as a metaphor for damage caused by structured and institutionalized violation. Dragon, steed, lizard, hare, eagle, hound, lion, unicorn are called upon, again as a sort of false benediction, as the unicorn is called upon to 'preserve the species', 'protect the species' (*I* 280), rather than a request for a deity to watch over individuals. (The idea of somebody watching over recurs again and again in McGuinness's work.) Through a belief in redemption, in the sacrifice of Christ and a consecration of the institutionalization of innocence, through the figure of the Virgin Mary, the Catholic Church shapes attitudes to damnation and redemption. Historically, the same church sometimes oversaw the systematic practice of violation within some institutions with a Catholic ethos and legitimized violation in the case of Ireland, with penitents working in Magdalene Laundries, something to which Patrica Burke-Brogan's play *Eclipsed* (1994) drew attention.

The work of Caravaggio resides between the torment of Medusa and the calm, poised excesses of Bacchus. Caravaggio's gift is to re-frame, to shift perspective, to re-imagine. With these things comes possibility. If the Cardinal can bring Caravaggio's brother back into his life, then the dream space, created by Lena (feminine), brings back his sister from the dead. Post-modern dramatic practice sometimes fails to differentiate between pain and pleasure and by so doing, leaves a whole unresolved blurring of elementary values. McGuinness blurs in order to contest and while laughter may be a defiance of pain, its ultimate goal is the pleasure of release.

Caravaggio is a mischief maker, who misappropriates the icons and symbols of the ruling order. Dream-play takes us into the underworld of the mind, and prostitution and poverty take an audience beyond the notions of art and artefact. Artifice gets us into the arena of performance and fluidity, artificiality into the world of codifications, improbable social discourse and etiquette, but both deliver perspectives on corruption. Beneath the reality of art resides dishonesty, beneath the reality of creativity resides destruction and beneath life there is death. What have these to do with innocence? There is nothing original about innocence. Innocence is fractured and incoherent and always catalyses into something else, in such a way that meaning is constantly postponed. Reality is insolvent. Innocence provides no enabling function, but a disabling one. It is restrictive, inhibitive and is a fallacy. Innocence must be regarded as performative, for performance implodes the term. Instead of internalizing innocence as a mode of being, what would happen if damnation instead is internalized? Yeats's lines in 'The Second Coming' are appropriate: 'The blood-dimmed tide is loosed, and everywhere/ The ceremony of innocence is drowned'.[27] In Fugard's *Dimetos*, the play ends with Dimetos laughing madly, with laughter as punishment. *Innocence* ends with the loud subversive laughter of Caravaggio. Ultimately the ambivalence of laughter generates misrule and protest and further complicates the concept of innocence. Laughter is defiance and the freeing energy here in this play: it is the laughter of the body and the physical release of laughter, not a holy laughter, but a mirth without any degree of transcendence. Through laughter, innocence proves to be unstable, unruly, as a profane, anarchic innocence is released. All borders and distinctions are transgressed. Art is neither ideologically neutral nor innocent. Metamorphosis and metatheatricality and mutation combine. As such, laughter as much as innocence is the gateway, through the 'rough trade' of reality and the rough trade of art and through, as a consequence, the centring of the dispossessed and the masquerade of the damned. This is what makes innocence so 'radical', unlike the way that innocence is naively appropriated as a way of calibrating meaning which is at the core of so much of contemporary Irish dramaturgy.

[1] W. B. Yeats, 'A Prayer for My Daughter' in Collected Poems (London: Picador, 1990), p.213.
[2] See Helen Lojek's Contexts for Frank McGuinness's Drama (Catholic University Press, forthcoming) for an extensive evaluation of the artist in McGuinness's work.
[3] All references to McGuinness's plays will be taken from Plays 1 and put in parentheses within the body of the text, unless otherwise stated.
[4] Joe Vanek suggests that the play Innocence was marked 'by a refusal to be frozen by anachronism - Innocence did not belong to a specific period' as the design 'incorporated Victorian fires, fifties chairs and a lot of modern junk' into an 'ostensibly Renaissance setting, thus ensuring that the play was seen not merely as a museum piece', 'In Conversation with Derek West', Theatre Ireland, 29, Autumn 1992, p.26.
[5] Caravaggio's 'revolutionary technique of tenebrism, or dramatic, selective illumination of form out of deep shadow, became a hallmark of Baroque painting. Scorning the traditional idealized

interpretation of religious subjects, he took his models from the streets and painted them realistically'.
Source:
http://www.kfki.hu/~arthp/bio/c/caravagg/biograph.html

6 McGuinness states in his 'Introduction' to *Plays 1*: 'I pieced together a fiction of his life based on a reading of the clues I imagined he'd left in his paintings ... I tried to make him a poet and in his poetry would be his painting. I used the city of Derry as my model for the Rome of his day ...' (London: Faber and Faber, 1996), p.xi.

7 Eamonn Jordan 'From Context to Text: The Construction of Innocence and Sexual Violation in Contemporary Irish Theatre', *Bullán: An Irish Studies Journal*, Summer/Fall 2001, p.51.

8 Hiroko Mikami, *Frank McGuinness and His Theatre of Paradox* (Gerrards Cross: Colin Smythe, 2002), p.54.

9 ibid., p.55.

10 BBC Interview. 1 May 1987. Quoted in Mikami, p.70.

11 Speaking of the 1980s, McGuinness argues: 'It is irony that destroys our claims to innocence. It is time to face experience. The poet William Blake wrote songs of innocence and experience. Is he a model for the writer in contemporary Ireland? Do we need a visionary radical with the propensity for seeing angels? No, so the time is not right for another De Valera ... Innocent? We're in it, up to our necks'. Frank McGuinness 'I am not confident for my country's future', *The Irish Times*, 25 December, 1989, p.8.

12 Program note, quoted by Mikami, p.59.

13 The red cloak appears in The Crucifixion of St. Peter, Judith Beheading Holofernes, Supper at Emmaus, The Deposition, Rest on Flight to Egypt, The Taking of Christ, Madonna del Rosario and The Death of the Virgin. Both the horse and the cloak appear in The Conversion on the Way to Damascus, and in St. Jerome the skull and cloak appear.

14 See Derek Jarman's filmscript, *Caravaggio* (London: Thames and Hudson, 1986). Jarman's film uses some of the techniques to reframe the works of Caravaggio that McGuinness also utilises.

15 '*The Death of the Virgin* was refused by the Carmelites because of the indignity of the Virgin's plebeian features, bared legs, and swollen belly'. Source:
http://www.kfki.hu/~arthp/bio/c/caravagg/biograph.html

16 In the painting *St. John the Baptist* the Youth with the Ram serves as a homoerotic image, as does the naked child Jesus standing on snake in *Madonna with the Serpent*.
17 Cooper notes that Caravaggio in the painting *The Conversion of St. Paul* 'used an image of physical and earthly passion, posing him [Paul] in the physical position of the receptive partner in homosexual love making' in *The Sexual Perspective: Homosexuality and Art in the Last 100 Years in the West* (London: Routledge and Keegan Paul, 1986), p.20-21.
18 Frank McGuinness discussing 'The Arts and Ideology' in *Crane Bag*, 9.2, 1985, p.66.
19 http://www.kfki.hu/~arthp/bio/c/caravagg/biograph.htm
20 'Lucio: See us. Whore: Touch us. Antonio: Paint us' (*I* 276). This offers further elaboration.
21 This moment is a substantial revision of the initial published version of text. *Innocence* (London: Faber and Faber, 1987).
22 Thomas Murphy deploys a similar image of inversion with the goat inheriting the kingdom of God in *The Sanctuary Lamp* (Dublin: Gallery Press, 1984), p.72.
23 In mythology, the unicorn, apart for the obvious phallic association, is symbol of purity, innocence and love and only the purest mortals are capable of seeing them. Only a virgin could capture it. Here, not only is the unicorn deified in a way, as it seen as a protector, but its association with innocence is shattered by the suggestion that the unicorn is no more than a goat and that Lena is a whore rather than a virgin. There is nothing to be gained by the pretence of innocence. The sense of doubleness brings all kinds of ambiguity.
24 McGuinness mentioned this to me during an unpublished interview 5 January 1993.
25 Jordan, op. cit., p.51.
26 The play can be partially read as a reworking of William Blake's poems the *Auguries of Innocence* and *Songs of Innocence*. ('For he hears the lamb's innocent call').
27 W. B. Yeats, 'The Second Coming' in *Collected Poems*, op. cit., p.211.

Derry Comes to Mid-Michigan: Staging *Carthaginians* at CMU
Timothy D. Connors

During the Fall of 1998 I was on sabbatical leave in Dublin from my position as Director of University Theatre at Central Michigan University. My purpose in being in Dublin was to research theatre education and training in Ireland – essentially I was looking for methods, styles and scripts to 'steal' for my own use back home. For the better part of sixteen weeks I attended an average of two plays per week, sat in on undergraduate classes at the Samuel Beckett Centre at Trinity College, and was allowed to participate in the MA in Drama Studies program at University College Dublin. During those sixteen weeks I repeatedly asked the same questions of everyone I met – students, faculty, actors, literary managers, directors: What plays/playwrights would you recommend American students read? What plays/playwrights would you recommend for production by American university students? Not surprisingly, the answers ranged from the usual suspects to the vaguely familiar to the totally – to me at least – unknown: Barry, Beckett, Behan, Boyd, Carr, Devlin, Farrell, Friel, Hughes, Keane, Kilroy, Leonard, Mac Intyre, McDonough, McGuinness, Meehan, Molloy, Moxley, Murphy (Jimmy), Murphy (Tom), O'Casey, O'Kelly, Riordan, Synge, Yeats. Each time I encountered an Irish play in the theatre I found myself cataloguing the production possibilities and problems for my students, my audience and myself. So what if many Dubliners I and myself. So what if many Dubliners I talked to disparaged Boucicault's *The Colleen Bawn* as 'the Abbey's tourist production' – could we do it at CMU? So what if the politics and style of Michael Harding's *Amazing Grace* were a bit obscure for American undergraduate students – should we do it at CMU? So what if the story and language of the stage adaptation of Flann O'Brien's novel *At Swim-Two-Birds* seemed virtually incomprehensible at first glance – would I like to do it at CMU?

At this point it might be helpful to know just a bit about the state of Michigan, the city of Mount Pleasant and CMU. Michigan is one of the twelve states generally referred to in the U. S. as the Midwest. It is composed of two peninsulas surrounded by four of the five Great Lakes (the Upper Peninsula is roughly perpendicular to the northern tip of the Lower Peninsula – a line drawn through the centre of each would result in an upside down 'L'). The population of Michigan is roughly 2.6 times that of the Republic of Ireland, and its land mass is over 1.7 times that of Ireland. Mount Pleasant, located near the centre of the lower peninsula, is the county seat of Isabella County and has a permanent population of about 26,000. The surrounding area would best be described as rural. The two largest local employers are the Saginaw-Chippewa Indian Tribe (which operates a large and popular hotel/casino complex), and Central Michigan University. CMU has an on-campus enrolment of over 17,000, and offers bachelors, masters, and doctoral degrees in a wide variety of disciplines. The university does not have an Irish Studies program so contact with Irish history, politics, culture and the arts comes more from isolated courses, faculty and staff of Irish heritage or with specific expertise in Irish issues, and through artistic performances. The Mount Pleasant area does, however, have some strong Irish roots. In 1990 over 12.8% of the residents of the city of Mount Pleasant (and Union Township) listed their ancestry, either in whole or in part, as Irish or Scotch-Irish – a small increase over 1880 when 12.5% of the residents of the listed Ireland as their birth place or the birthplace of one or both of their parents. Even the athletic teams of Mount Pleasant's Sacred Heart Academy are known as 'the Irish'.

By the time I left Dublin for home, I had come to the conclusion – heavily influenced by the number of times they had been suggested to me but also based on having read a large number of Irish plays – that Marina Carr and Frank McGuinness held out the most promise (although Anne Devlin's *After Easter* remained a strong contender). I had seen and enjoyed Carr's *By the Bog of Cats* at the Abbey but CMU had produced Brendan Kennelly's version of *The Trojan Women* while I was on sabbatical and it seemed a bit too soon for *Medea* through the lens of the conflict between travellers and settled people. Perhaps *The Mai* or *Portia Coughlan*? No, *By the Bog of Cats* it would be – but not just yet.

The passion with which people whom I admired and respected spoke about Frank McGuinness kept me looking in his direction – *The Factory Girls*, *Observe the Sons of Ulster Marching Towards the Somme*, and *Carthaginians*. All three of these plays were appealing to me and all three seemed 'doable' in terms of technical demands, our production facilities and students actors. *Carthaginians* emerged a the front runner as much for practical reasons – e.g., a more gender balanced cast – as any other although I was convinced that the characters and subject matter of the play could prove to be accessible to both cast and audience. Once the play had been selected, I turned full attention to production preparations beginning, as always, with a question: how best to present this play (*Carthaginians*) in this space (Bush Theatre, a 500 seat modified proscenium arch theatre) with this cast (traditional aged – 18 to 22 year old – undergraduate students) for this audience (primarily composed of CMU faculty, staff and students with a healthy dose of community members)?

Very early in the preparation stage two crucial decisions were made about the look and sound of the play. The first had to do with the place of the play – Creggan Graveyard. Working with the CMU scenic and lighting designer, Bill Valle, it was decided not to attempt to recreate the look and feel of the actual Derry location. We opted instead for a simplified, almost presentational graveyard. The resulting ground plan was a strongly horizontal, two-level arrangement divided by a path that crossed the stage from right to left. Scattered about the stage were head stones and grave markers whose design was based on photographs of Irish cemeteries, and included large standing Celtic crosses positioned upstage behind a black scrim. The set was otherwise completely open and was backed by a blue cyc. The look, then, did not give a sense of forced enclosure – no walls, no gates, no physical obstacles to entering or leaving the graveyard. Instead, we were counting on the actors to create the sense of being trapped by their emotional turmoil rather than by the physical environment. (Costumes, designed by Doris Ramsey, were chosen for their realism. Dido's football uniform presented an interesting research challenge. All the props were also chosen for their realism. Lighting was generally realistic although it could be, and was, manipulated for focus and effect.)

The second decision had to do with the sound of the play – specifically, what kind of dialect would the actors speak? My stay in Dublin, travel around Ireland and exposure to Irish television and radio had made me keenly aware of the multitude of Irish dialects – 15 in Dublin alone according to one newspaper article I read shortly before coming home. I was determined that we would do neither Barry Fitzgerald nor the Lucky Charms leprechaun but beyond that I wasn't sure which way to go. I researched different possibilities – the excellent work being done by the International Dialects of English Archive (IDEA) at the University of Kansas, various dialect tapes, written descriptions of dialect sound substitutions, IPA sources, etc. Ultimately, I decided to work with the cast on a fairly generic Irish sound primarily based on the work of Jerry Blunt but adapted for ease of understanding as necessary. Two of my colleagues at the time – Robin Monteith and James Bunzli – developed a guide to Irish pronunciation using IPA to show vowel substitutions, etc. The goals in our dialect work were quite simply consistency within and between characters, and ease of understanding for the audience.

In researching background for the play, it became obvious that McGuinness, in general, and *Carthaginians*, in particular, were not well known nor widely produced in the U.S. outside of large metropolitan areas with significant Irish populations. I knew our production would not be a premier production but I was surprised to learn that a production was being done at Boston College that opened within a day or two of ours. I exchanged several e-mail messages related to the play, interpretation, staging difficulties, etc., with the director of that production. Because *Carthaginians* was an unknown to our students and because we auditioned on the second day of the semester, there was little chance that students auditioning for the production would have an opportunity to read the play in advance. I was also sure that the incident at the centre of the character's memories – Bloody Sunday – was unknown except as the title of a 'really neat U2 song' as more than one student remarked. Therefore, for auditions, I put together a one-page information sheet giving an introduction to both the real life background of the play and the fictional events. I also included brief descriptions of the characters:

> **Maela:** in her 40s; her daughter died of cancer on the day of Bloody Sunday; she has moved into the cemetery in the belief that if she (and others) believe hard enough, the dead will come back to life
> **Greta:** in her 30s; an only child, she spent much of her youth caring for her elderly parents (including her 'cracked' mother); she smokes
> **Sarah:** in her 30s; a recovering drug addict, she has been in love with Hark for a long time and is now determined to win him for herself
> **Dido:** in his 20s; openly gay in a society which is intolerant of homosexuality; in love with Hark
> **Hark:** in his 30s; active in the civil rights movement he was arrested, tortured and imprisoned for those activities
> **Paul:** in his 30s; he is building a 'monument' to the dead through which they will re-enter the world; a very intelligent young man
> **Seph:** in his 20s; questioned as a young man by the authorities, he 'named names' in order to get people arrested and, so he thought, into the safety of prison; plays guitar.

For general auditions I tried to choose audition scenes that included less 'information' about Bloody Sunday and focused more on character. For call-backs, I spent some time briefing the students on both actual and fictional previous events mentioned in the play and did not shy away from choosing scenes which depended much more heavily on a knowledge of Bloody Sunday and its aftermath (e.g., the scene between Hark and Dido in Scene Two in which Hark demonstrates interrogation techniques on Dido, and the end of Scene Seven when Paul recites the names of the dead).

One of the first things I did when casting was complete was give each actor a cassette tape of songs related to the play or 'the Troubles' or Irish history. The tape included songs explicitly called for or referred to in the text: 'We Shall Overcome,' 'Danny Boy,' Don McLean's 'Babylon,' and 'When I am laid' from *Dido and Aeneas*. I included several songs from an album entitled 'This is Free Belfast': 'Why Are the British Troops Here?' 'Burntollet Bridge Ambush,' 'Craig's Dragoons,' 'The Bogside Doodle Bug,' 'The Bogside Man,' 'Ballymurphy' and 'Up in the Armagh Prison'; lyrics for each of these songs were also given to the cast. The remainder of the tape was composed of songs taken from several CDs by The Wolfe Tones, Christy Moore and, of course, U2: 'No Time for Love,' 'The Impartial Police Force,' 'God Save Ireland,' 'Sunday Bloody Sunday,' 'Rifles of the IRA,' 'Long Kesh,' and 'The Broad Black Brimmer.' The majority of these songs – especially those by the Wolfe Tones and from 'This is Free Belfast' – were deliberately chosen for their political content, their anti-British or pro-Republican point of view. Many of these same songs were incorporated into the pre-show, intermission and post-show music.

In early meetings with the cast I spent a fair bit of time providing background information about 'the Troubles'. Since no one in the cast had heard of McGuinness before the play was announced for the season, and since the majority of them knew little or almost nothing about 'the Troubles', I developed handouts for them giving a brief outline history of Ireland. I also drew heavily from the 'Path to Peace' website hosted and maintained by *The Irish Times* (http://www.ireland.com/special/peace/index.htm) for background information, then current views and news of Bloody Sunday and photographs, as well as books such as Raymond McClean's *The Road to Bloody Sunday* (1977) and Don Mullan's compilation of eyewitness accounts, *Bloody Sunday: Massacre in Northern Ireland* (1997). Other sources which proved helpful include *Ireland: A Social and Cultural History, 1922 to the Present* by Terence Brown (1985), *Postnationalist Ireland: Politics, Culture, Philosophy* by Richard Kearney (1997), G. R. Sloan's *The Geopolitics of Anglo-Irish Relations in the Twentieth Century* (1997), *The Irish Question: Two Centuries of Conflict* by Lawrence J. McCaffrey (1995), and Feargal Cochrane's *Unionist Politics and the Politics of Unionism Since the Anglo-Irish Agreement* (1997). At one early session with the cast, we watched a PBS video entitled 'The Road to Bloody Sunday: How the Troubles in Northern Ireland Began' which put sound and faces to the participants and incidents. I also put together a PowerPoint presentation of images from the events of Bloody Sunday (and more contemporary images of Derry) that I gathered from a number of print and web sources. This background material made it much easier for the cast to understand, at least intellectually, the historical/political contexts of the play.

As an actor and director, I am a firm believer in research to support analysis of characters and text. I am, however, equally firm in my belief that actors and directors should not 'stage' their research, they should stage the play. The task at hand, then, shifted from developing context to developing a sense of character and story contained in the text. I took as my starting point a brief exchange between Hark and Dido from near the end of the play:

> **Hark:** You would have been only a kid, Dido.
> **Dido:** There were no kids after Bloody Sunday.[1]

(This line strongly parallels McGuinness's own reaction to Bloody Sunday: 'My adolescence ended that day.'[2]) Dido's line suggests loss – of innocence, at the very least, but also of things both more tangible and more elusive as well. Beginning with the character descriptions I used at auditions, the cast and I began to explore the details of the tangible losses of the characters, including those losses not directly related to Bloody Sunday: Maela's child, Paul's grasp on reality, Seph's place among his former comrades, Greta's ability to have children, Hark's ability to feel, etc. Only Dido seems not to have lost something as a direct result of Bloody Sunday (he clearly feels lost but the cause seems less to do with 30 January 1972 than with his personal struggle to find a place in society). As the 'facts' of the story, character relationships and backgrounds became clearer for most of the characters, the function(s) of Dido became somewhat less clear. For example, while Paul and Hark are seemingly quite able to come and go from the graveyard, it is Dido who acts as the real emissary to and from the outside world for all of them – he does the shopping, brings news and entertainment, and, ultimately, resolution to the play. But why Dido? Because he has always been apart from the others? Because he has always been different in a society which seems to demand a certain kind of religious/political conformity? Perhaps it is because Dido was not really part of Bloody Sunday but of the generation which followed, the generation which heard the stories and saw the pictures and felt the pain but which also wants to move forward without forgetting, wants to resolve (but not necessarily absolve). Or, perhaps, none of the action of the play is 'real' – all the characters are literal 'inhabitants' of the graveyard and it is Dido's job to bring them to the point where they can forgive themselves their shortcomings and, in so doing, achieve eternal rest. (It was only recently, when I asked cast members about their experience with the play, that I found out that several of them had spent some time together sitting in a local graveyard 'absorbing atmosphere', I presume, and wondering about the 'existence' of their characters.) Jason Nostrant, the actor who played Dido, had much the same sense when he first read the play, especially in light of the Dido's spreading flowers over the sleeping characters and his references to Carthage.

I was lucky enough to have a cast that was able to grasp their characters in both an intellectual and emotional manner. I was especially pleased, in rehearsal and performance, with the way in which they handled the storytelling demands of the play (e.g., the 'details' of Bloody Sunday and their involvement or lack thereof in the event) and the emotional content of the characters. Each was able to achieve an understanding that made their individual 'confessionals' – e.g., Sarah's (Kendrah McKay) acknowledgement of her drug addiction and prostitution to feed her habit; Seph's (Christopher Palazzolo) 'war in his head'; Maela's (Tiffany Soule) reliving of the day her daughter died; Greta's (Dianna Schoenborn) feeling of inadequacy and fear of being alone; Paul's (Christopher Johnston) traumatic response to the body bags used for the dead on Bloody Sunday; Hark's (Jeffrey Sanders) admission of the cowardice that prevented him from using his gun to defend his comrades when ambushed – believable and poignant. In some ways, it was the smaller moments and nuances of relationship which proved more difficult for the actors – e.g., Dido's relationship to Sarah, Greta's use of rhyme ('Charlie, Charlie, chuck-chuck-chuck. Went to bed with three wee ducks.'[3]), Paul's pyramid, Hark's 'Flintstones' references, Seph's decision to break his silence.

Throughout the rehearsal period there were other elements and moments of the play that I had concerns about/difficulties with. The three biggest of those concerns were: (1) how would an audience unfamiliar with the details of Bloody Sunday react to the play? (2) how should we handle Paul's litany of the dead? and (3) how to present the last two pages of the script (from immediately after Paul's listing of the dead through Dido's final monologue)? The first concern was one that I knew could not be easily solved. Every piece of publicity about the play gave a brief recounting of the events surrounding Bloody Sunday. While I am not a big fan of programme notes – too often they seem like a director's apology for what s/he intended to do rather than what they got to happen on stage – I included one for this production. The programme note addressed two issues – the historical background of the events of Bloody Sunday, and 'smoking' in the production. (Like many universities, CMU has a strict no-smoking policy in all campus buildings. Although dramatic presentations are explicitly exempt from this prohibition, I have grown increasingly uncomfortable with asking actors to learn to smoke for the sake of character. Instead, I opted for a convention in which real cigarettes and matches/lighters were used, the tobacco was never lit but the actors still performed the rituals of smoking – inhaling/exhaling, flicking ashes, stubbing out, etc.). I knew that many of our audience would not take the time to read the programme notes beforehand so I was not counting on the notes to provide background. Instead, I looked for textual references that pointed toward the 'history' and worked to make sure that those moments were clearly told. Two role-playing sequences were particularly effective in establishing both background and character attitudes. The first of these is in Scene Three when Greta and Hark lead the others into singing 'We Shall Overcome.' Because of the intimate connection between the Civil Rights movement in the U.S. and this song – a song that is in some way familiar to our entire audience – an immediate parallel is established in the audience's mind between events/attitudes here and those in Northern Ireland. When Hark adopts his American accent for the 'Brothers and sisters, I have a dream' sequence[4] he also immediately taps into a social/political iconography familiar to all Americans. Again, the use of a reference point widely familiar to an American audience – even one as young as ours – helped them see the similarities in situation and passion. The other, and much more extended, role-playing sequence is Dido's play in Scene Four – 'The Burning Balaclava.' Although this section of the play presents 'the Troubles' in a simplified, stereotypical (and wonderfully satiric) way, it was very successful in performance in giving a broad introduction to the attitudes of many of the residents of Derry in a way our audience could understand and appreciate.

    The next major area of concern for me was Paul's recitation of the names, ages and addresses of the dead from Bloody Sunday. This moment in the play is so event-specific that I was unsure how the audience would respond to the list of actual people about whom they knew virtually nothing. The listing also seems to interrupt the flow of the play – my first impression was that it brought the play to a dead halt. Obviously, the impact of this moment on an Irish audience would be much greater than anything we could hope to accomplish at CMU. In my mind, I equated this moment to the recitation of the names of those lost in Vietnam and/or to AIDS. For a Michigan audience there was also a parallel to the ritual ringing of bells to mark the loss/remembrance of victims of shipwrecks on the Great Lakes. In working with the actor playing Paul (Christopher Johnston), we concentrated on making the names as personal as possible. I was extremely fortunate in that Johnston was able to give each person mentioned a different emphasis, one time acknowledging the youth of the victim, the next their address, and another time their name – he invited us to remember with him these people who were his/our friends or neighbours or relatives. Through his ability to personalize the recitation of names, Johnson was also able to communicate the collective sense of loss of the Derry community in a most immediate and powerful way. The simplicity and honesty of this led nicely into the almost chorus-like next few lines in which the characters urge themselves (and us) to raise/wash/bury the dead and, most importantly, to forgive. Paul's recitation and the company lines immediately following were staged in a fairly presentational manner. Paul began to name the victims in a position USR and addressing the other characters. As he continued, he moved downstage and turned toward the audience (lighting also changed to provide additional focus on Paul). By the time Paul was finished, he was directly addressing the audience without any attempt to deny the overt theatricality of the moment. During the course of the next sequence of lines, the other characters also moved into positions in which they, too, were facing straight out into the audience as they both invited and implored the audience to understand their pain and sorrow, their need to remember and inability to forget:

> **Dido:** Do you see the dead?
> **Greta:** The dead beside you.
> **Maela:** The dead behind you.
> **Sarah:** The dead before you.

Greta: Forgive the dead.
Maela: Forgive the dying.
Sarah: Forgive the living.
Paul: Forgive yourself.
Hark: Forgive yourself.
Seph: Forgive yourself.
Maela: Bury the dead.
Greta: Raise the dying.
Sarah: Wash the living.[5]

The inclusion of the audience at this moment seemed of vital importance to me, especially if we were going to make the point of the collective loss but also collective responsibility which characters (and, implicitly, audience) share.

Finally, the last speech of the play – Dido's monologue as he wanders among the other characters as they lie down to rest/sleep in graveyard – was an enigma from the beginning. On what level of reality/unreality should this scene be approached? Is it an integral part of the action of the play or more like a *coda*? And exactly who/what is Dido instructing to 'Play'?[6] At this point in the play, Dido seems to shift from being simply another one of the characters to a position just short of complete omniscience. Why is it Dido, the youngest of the characters and the one seemingly least directly affected by Bloody Sunday, who offers his 'elders' a form of absolution through peaceful sleep? I took the position that Dido represents a kind of bridge between past and future – he was 'there' on Bloody Sunday but his life will be lived beyond the physical and emotional constraints of the past. Dido will neither deny nor forget the past but he is also determined to seek a life in a 'new' Derry, one not defined solely by religion (or sexual orientation). In this interpretation, Dido is a symbol of hope – hope deferred or delayed but still possible.

Following the production, I visited some classes that had been required to attend a performance. The questions most frequently asked had to do with the social/political background of the play. Next most frequent were questions related to the title of the play (no easy answer to this one – thanks a lot Mr. McGuinness!) and the 'difficulty' of getting an actor to play gay (this question took me totally by surprise; it never occurred to me because it never seemed to be a problem for any of us involved in the production)⁷. Other questions had to do with the reasons for selecting the play and technical difficulties – e.g., ground plan, props, etc.⁸ My own questions about the production were divided between technical issues (e.g., inconsistencies in accent, 'smoking,' the look and texture of the sausage Dido smears over Hark's chest, size and material of Paul's pyramid) and interpretive choices (e.g., to what extent is Dido actually in love with Hark, why is Seph allowed to remain a part of/forced apart from the rest, how mad are Maela and Paul).

Carthaginians marked the beginning of what I'm sure is going to be a long, personal odyssey through Irish dramatic literature. Since this 1999 production I have also directed Beckett's *Endgame* (February 2002) and am involved in pre-production research for a November 2002 production of *The Playboy of the Western World*. While I have not and will not abandon drama from other parts of the world (including home-grown original works I find so exciting), I do find my list of 'must-do' Irish playwrights growing at a faster pace than those from any other region or country – in my little corner of the world they seem to have a playability and relevance so important to my work as a theatre educator and director.

[1] Frank McGuinness, *Plays 1* (London: Faber and Faber, 1996), p.377.
[2] McGuinness, p.xi.
[3] McGuinness, p.309.
[4] McGuinness, pp.322-323.
[5] McGuinness, pp.378-379.
[6] McGuinness, p.379.
[7] These questions occurred most in theatre appreciation classes composed primarily of students with limited or no experience of live theatre.
[8] These questions came primarily from students enrolled in beginning directing classes.

Carthaginians: Narratives of Death and Resurrection in a Derry Graveyard
Anne F. Kelly-O'Reilly

Reading and re-reading *Carthaginians* I am reminded of a passage in the novel *Night* by Elie Weisel, a Jewish survivor of the holocaust.

> The SS hung two Jewish men and a boy before the assembled inhabitants of the camp. The men died quickly but the death struggle of the boy lasted half an hour. 'Where is God? Where is he?' a man behind me asked. I heard the man cry again 'Where is God now?' and I heard a voice within me answer, 'Here he is – he is hanging there on the gallows.' [1]

Frank McGuinness's play, *Carthaginians*, could be subtitled 'Where is God?' or more accurately 'Where was God?' when on Bloody Sunday (1972), thirteen innocent people, marching for Civil Rights, were gunned down and killed. The play set in 1988 is set in a graveyard, where a group of people await the resurrection of the dead. Each of them has been touched in different ways by the horror of what happened on that fateful day. Each carries the horror and trauma within them. The play is about suffering and pain, about loss of innocence and hope, about death in all its guises. The play is about memory – about remembering what has been repressed or forgotten or denied.

> Pathologies of memory are characteristic features of post-traumatic stress disorder (PTSD). These range from amnesia for part, or all, of the traumatic events to frank dissociation,

in which large realms of experience or aspects of one's identity are disowned. Such failures of recall can *paradoxically coexist* with the opposite: intruding memories and unbidden repetitive images of traumatic events. ²

It is about a vision of hell that needs and cries out for a vision of resurrection. It can be read as a contemporary Passion narrative. The brutal obscenity of death by crucifixion is mirrored in the obscenity of the murders on Bloody Sunday. If crucifixion can be interpreted as humanity at the zero point, forsaken by the divine, so too can the events of Bloody Sunday. How can such a story be told? How can one forgive oneself for having survived? What kind of reconciliation is possible between the warring communities and the warring aspects of the individual human psyche? What can heal such splitting apart? The hope of resurrection – of passing from death to life – is the journey of the play. It unfolds in the liminal or threshold space of a graveyard.

> The graveyard, hiding place in time gone by for outcasts, lepers, fugitives, the insane; shunned by the living because of their fear of the dead; becomes for McGuinness another borderland. The watchers have moved into this borderland under the stress of loss or guilt.³

From the Wednesday to the Sunday morning the characters will face the demons of the past, as they tell their stories. Their city, like Carthage, has been destroyed, as has each of their lives. In the womb-tomb space of the graveyard they will play and sing and ritualize their way towards a new imagining. The alternative sacred space of theatre will facilitate a coming home, a transformation both for the characters and the audience, in their transition from death to life.

I propose to consider the play as a contemporary passion narrative, and will interpret the unfolding days of the play as a mirroring of the traditional Holy Week in the Christian calendar, as the community prepared for Easter. Liturgically in the Catholic tradition the ceremonies of Holy Week set before the participants the events leading up to the crucifixion and resurrection of Jesus. In the sacred space of ritual and story participants are invited through a state of heightened awareness to journey the way of the Cross with Jesus. Christians are called to feel his suffering and pain, to identify with it and in so doing to experience their own suffering and grief transformed. The journey of Holy Week is a journey towards the glory and joy of resurrection. The play *Carthaginians* places this same journey from death to life, in a secular setting, where there is no promise of salvation from outside, and the characters are called to be saviours of themselves and each other.

The women, Maela, Greta and Sarah, have had a vision: 'what the three of us have seen, Maela.'[4] They believe that the dead will rise. They have come to keep vigil in the graveyard, to wait for the miracle to happen. They have been joined by three men, Paul, Seph and Hark. The seventh character, Dido, is a homosexual who is a type of Mother Courage figure at one level and at another he plays a transgressive role as the transvestite playwright, Fionnuala McGonigle. While the play is ostensibly realist the question of the women's vision alongside the interruptive presence of Dido pushes against the boundaries of the realist frame. It will be further fractured and questioned by Dido's play *The Burning Balaclava*, where characters play different parts and different genders and Dido himself (playwright Fionnuala) plays two distinct roles as a tormented female martyr figure and a nameless British soldier. The play within the play stretches the realist parameters in its content and performance. Dirty jokes, snatches of song, remembered poetry, nursery rhymes, football chants and talk about the Western genre of cinema suggest an inter-textual reality within which the play (as a whole) operates. There is no seamless narrative of events but rather a series of dissociated voices consequent on the experience of trauma.

> The traumatised, we might say, carry an impossible history within them, or they become themselves the symptom of a history that they cannot entirely possess.[5]

The deep wounding that has occurred in the light of such trauma is in the generative or feeling function of the human being. Seph is so wounded (because of his informing) that he does not speak at all for most of the play. Maela's pain at the death of her daughter from cancer has left her locked and frozen in her denial and unable to move forward. Sarah has lived as a junkie and prostitute in Holland for years, and now wants a child. Hark who has been in prison and now works as a gravedigger feels that the person he was nine years ago (Johnnie) no longer exists. Paul retreats into periods of madness as a way of coping, while he builds his pyramid for the dead, out of the rubbish of the town. Greta has had an operation that makes her feel unwomanly and unable to bear children. (A hysterectomy, I presume). Their respective wounds make it impossible for them to be life givers, either to themselves or of others.

The dirty jokes they share are often about sex and sexuality – where the wound seems deepest. (A similar theme runs through *Innocence*.) The man whose penis falls off, the different female approaches to the male sex organ, or Maela's failed joke about the woman with the pain in her child, are further manifestations of the wound in the generative or feeling function.

Maela has been putting clothes on her daughter's grave as if dressing her. She is saving for her birthday, believing 'she's not dead, you know' (C 300). Dido enters wheeling a pram, in which he stores the supplies that the others have ordered. His singing of a section from *Danny Boy* which ends with 'kneel and say an Ave there pour moi' (*C* 301) alerts us to where he is coming from. The camp performance with the pram and the song, and later in drag, while foregrounding homosexuality, also draws attention to the interpretative frameworks within which one experiences history. Dido's position (similar to Pyper's in *Observe the Sons of Ulster*) offers us the vantage point of the outsider and provides 'a useful perspective – a distance from which events, philosophies, social and moral issues may be evaluated.'[6]

The outsider position of the homosexual questions perceived assumptions, not simply about compulsory heterosexuality, but about our ways of knowing. It also brings a 'freshness into drama' by 'cutting through the stale rhetoric and inadequate analysis of unthinking, powerful insiders.'[7] Dido is making money in his transactions, has moved into Maela's home and is selling their story to the newspapers. Greta reads:

> 'The girls may be suffering from illusions,' Mr. Martin added. 'They are simple but sincere souls, and each has endured a great personal tragedy,' he concluded. We say good luck, Ghostbusters, and if the dead rise, let us know.
> **Dido:** Typical, typical. I'm doing my best. I need to rouse national interest. Nobody believes you in Derry, they think you're lunatics. The Catholics think you're mad, and the Prods think you're Martians.
> **Maela:** Who cares what anybody thinks as long as we believe it? (*C* 306-7)

Whatever the original vision, it is not validated by those outside who dismiss it according to their own paradigms. Greta in Anne Devlin's *After Easter* faces similar rejection when she tries to find a way of validating her own visionary experiences. Similar to Greta's sisters the three women in this play support one another, thus authenticating what the other has experienced. Dido is making a collection of pressed flowers, believing that 'Flowers are more gentle when they're dead' (*C* 308) and adverting to their magical properties. Paul enters, reminiscent of an Old Testament Jeremiah. As seer, he has become slightly unhinged. His greeting while addressed to the town of Derry is actually applicable to the characters we have just met. ('Pack of whores. Pack of queers. Pack of traitors' [*C* 308].) He recalls the early Irish Christian Saint Malachy who had a vision of the end of the world, within which Derry was included. Paul believes that he too can see like Malachy, and blames him for not stopping his prophesy.

> **Paul:** St. Malachy. He saw the end of the world. He prophesied it. He saw the waters rise over Derry. He saw the Foyle and Swilly meet, and that will be Derry gone. He saw it, but will he stop it? No. He sees the state of this town, but so do I see it. And I will search every dump in this town for rubbish. I'm building a pyramid. When the dead rise, I'll walk into the pyramid with them and walk away from this town and the state it's in. And if I find St. Malachy hiding in this city, I'll kill him, I'll kill him, I'll knock his teeth down his

throat. (*Paul exits.*)
Maela: Poor St.Malachy. (*C* 308)

Paul's experience of the destruction of Derry and its people on Bloody Sunday leaves him in a similar role as a prophet of doom. He has seen the 'rubbishing' of all that he held sacred and precious and a monument made of rubbish will become a fitting testimony. The prophet in the Hebrew tradition was the one who grieved, that a new future might emerge. Through the work of his own hands he will build a pyramid through which the 'dead will find their way back to this world' (*C* 320). Maela continues to knit, reminiscent of the French woman at the guillotine.

Greta's inability to save the injured bird serves as an object of transference and brings us closer to the pain she is carrying. Throughout the play she will recite snatches of the rhyme, 'Charlie, Charlie, chuck-chuck-chuck.' Her wound is in her inner female self. She cannot sleep, nor can Paul. He talks of having been at a quiz but said nothing. 'I used to run it. Questions and answers' (*C* 309). It is almost as if life has become too painful to fit into the categories it once fitted into. Virgil's leading of Dante through the city of hell can no longer be contained within the parameters of the quiz-game. Now the question Paul asks is 'Who will guide me through this city of hell?' (*C* 309). Derry has become foreign to him and he likens it to the ancient city of Carthage, a city similar in size to Derry and ruled and destroyed by a great Empire. Paul's myth of origins is to locate himself as a Carthaginian, 'sitting in the ruins, in the graveyard.' (*C* 310) His sense of belonging to the place and the earth transcends the claims of empires: 'But I'm no slave. I am Carthaginian. This earth is mine, not Britain's, not Rome's. Mine' (*C* 311). Equally his remembering has mythic dimensions: 'Virgil led Dante through the city of hell and Dante said that to remember times of happiness in times of great woe, that's the sorrow beyond enduring' (*C* 311).

The violence of the scene between Hark and Dido is disturbing in its use of sexual imagery. Just as the army had picked up Hark, he mirrors this in pretending to pick up Dido. Hark's abhorrence of the sexuality of the gay man is as abhorrent as the imagined English soldier's image of a united Ireland. 'What happens when cocks unite? Disease, boy, disease. The united Ireland's your disease' (*C* 314). Dido's response continues to develop this sexual imagery : 'Some people here fuck with a bullet and the rest fuck with a Bible, but I belong to neither ...' (*C* 315). The sublimation of sexual energy through religion or violence is a familiar theme, again highlighting the wounded feeling function. Later Hark will make reference, again in conversation with Dido, as to whether the British Army 'strip-searched' him (*C* 323) and whether he enjoyed it.

Hark while refusing to acknowledge continuity with what he once was ('Johnny is dead' [*C* 316]) is also fearful of relationship with Sarah, having been hurt before. He wants to hurt her through his singing of the song about the whores in Amsterdam. Sighting the dead bird, he feels pity, the 'poor bird' (*C* 317). This moment of compassion is the beginning of his journey back to himself.

A question running through the play is whether the characters can continue to hope, and just what kind of hope is possible. Whether hope and history can indeed rhyme is a fundamental question. Each of their lives has been changed radically through death, loss, betrayal, imprisonment. Hark's voice as the realism of the gravedigger promises no hope in the resurrection of the dead. Paul follows the stars as he has to have faith in something while Greta suggests that he 'should have faith in yourself.' Greta feels too tired to have faith, and Hark hearing 'the cry of a lost soul' (*C* 321) asks her (parody of the concerned priest) why she has abandoned hope and turned her back on the faith of her childhood. Greta humorously answers that 'I blame it on television myself' (*C* 321).

The 'wit and wisdom' of Derry unite them in their singing of 'We shall overcome' which leads into a parody of Martin Luther King's famous speech 'I have a dream'. In contrast to his vision of unity theirs is one of separation.

Hark: Catholics shall stand with Catholics, Protestants with Protestants –

> **Maela:** Should it not be 'Catholics will stand with Protestants.'?
> **Hark:** I speak of dreams, sister, not of insanity. Let us be like the asshole and let us be apart. (*C* 323)

The inversion of the dream and the crudeness of the imagery work in a subversive way, questioning and overturning all preconceptions of what unity might mean. The subsequent prayer is a similar inversion alerting us to the definition of self and other through hatred and bigotry, that is needed to maintain separate identities.

> **Greta:** Hallulia.
> **Hark:** Let us live apart as we choose to live apart. Let us hate as we wish to hate.
> **Greta:** Hallulia, brother.
> **Hark:** Let us wander forth into the wilderness of bigotry and let us spread more bigotry. Let us create a nation fit for assholes to live in. For as assholes we are known to each other and like the asshole let us forever remain apart. (*C* 323)

A strange incident between Hark and Dido occurs when Dido returns to the graveyard with provisions. He has brought some sausages which he mashes into Hark's chest and then his face. He then produces a 'face-cloth, basin, flask of hot water, stool and shirt' (*C* 324) from his pram and proceeds to wash and clean Hark's chest. This ritual bathing has echoes of the ritual at the Last Supper when Jesus washed the feet of his disciples, one of whom went out to betray him. It is one of the moments celebrated in the Holy Thursday liturgy during Holy Week, and echoes John's gospel where Jesus calls his disciples friends rather than servants. This scene represents an inversion of the ritual where Dido defiles Hark in revenge and then cleanses him in a gesture of reconciliation. While cleaning Hark's chest he 'tweaks Hark's nipple' as illustration of 'where the future lies, sado-masochism' (*C* 325). While his reference is explicitly to behaviour within homosexual relationships the Derry wit sees it in another way as a description of marriage.

> **Dido:** You fancy someone, you take them to bed, you beat the shite out of them.

> **Maela:** I see. Marriage.
> **Dido:** Not exactly. There's pleasure in sado-masochism.
> (*C* 325)

The blurring of the lines between pleasure and pain are a continuation of the sexual theme already introduced in the Hark/Dido exchange (*C* 314-315). The rituals of war, sado-masochism and sport seem to validate the one patriarchal aesthetic. Dido relates an encounter with a Lebanese, who was wandering through Derry:

> He said, 'Listen, listen to the earth. The earth can speak. It says, Cease your violent hand. I who gave birth to you will bring death to you. Cease your violent hand. That is my dream. I pray my dream comes true.' (*C* 326)

Dido can only translate this into a desire that Derry City will win the European Cup – a dream that seems just as impossible. The vision of a cessation of violence cannot be grounded. The only dream that he might have an inkling of how to realize would be to build up the local football team. Sarah cannot be stopped from telling her story (compare *Baglady* and *The Bread Man*), even though people around her might try to stop her. Her journey through addiction is a story of a journey from death to life. Like the fairytale of *The Handless Maiden* she eventually saves herself by the strength of her own hands, rather than those of another.

> I walked by the canals of Amsterdam. I was sinking under the weight of powder. I sank and I sank until I felt hands lift me. I thought they were yours, Hark, but they were my own. I saved myself, Johnny. I saw myself dead in Amsterdam. I've come back from the dead. I'm clean.
>
> Clean. It's true. And if what we saw is true, if the dead are to rise again, then we must tell each other the truth. For us all to rise again. (C 328)

Telling the truth rather than colluding with a culture of lies or silence is the way towards redemption. The community gathered in the graveyard can enable each other to hear the truth of their lives.

Scene four introduces Dido's play, written by his alias, French woman Fionnula McGonigle who changed her name in sympathy with Derry people whose city also had its name changed. The play is a contribution to the resistance. The text of the play is distributed along with props. All the characters' names are variations on Doherty (Mrs. Doherty, Padraig O'Dochartaigh, Mercy Dogherty, Father Docherty, Jimmy Doherty), the British soldier is nameless. Props include stolen balaclavas, a headscarf and apron, a statue of the Sacred Heart, water pistols for everyone, a Tricolour and a large flag pin, rosary beads and a crucifix, a flat cap, two white sheets, a stuffed dog on a lead, a helmet and toy rifle. Most of the characters are tormented in one way or another.

While the similarity in the names suggests that very little separates the characters, the play parodies religious bigotry and political ideology. All of the characters end up dead, even the dog, the wee hound of Ulster which firmly knocks the Cuchulainn myth off its pedestal. The theme of the long suffering Irish mother who gives up her children to war is also parodied. (Compare O'Casey's Juno, for example.) The symbols that define the characters in religious and political terms are easily recognized as they are distributed amongst the characters. The ambiguity of symbols is raised for the audience as the excesses and abuses evoked by them lead to more and more violence. It focuses attention on how much of the war in Northern Ireland is in fact a war about symbols and how and what they mean. The easy stereotyping of the other through the use of symbols in the play allows the audience to see the power of symbols at work in a community. The war over symbols suggests a collapse of the symbolic function into literalism. When the real ambiguity and ambivalence of symbols is denied, the resultant literalism ultimately leads to the death of the symbol, at least in its more liberating aspects. When a symbol ceases to function in an open-ended symbolic way but collapses into a banal literalism it functions in a diabolic way, tearing people apart, and may result in violence and death. Official religion, represented in this play by the silent Catholic priest, who speaks by waving white flags, in the Waterside area of the city (compare Father Edward Daly) is ultimately powerless against the community's misappropriation of the symbolic function.

As the characters fall around laughing after the performance of the play, agreeing it was 'shite' (*C* 344), Seph speaks and asks for a cigarette. The ritual space of play has permitted all kinds of transgression. Seph, who has been an informer, now feels allowed to speak about what he saw on Bloody Sunday. A space of remembering has been opened up by the play. It facilitates access to a memory repressed or denied. through offering another vantage point of interpretation of the events of history. Each character will gradually come to transform their traumatic memory of events into a narrative one.

Scene five takes us further into Friday and deeper into remembering. As Greta and Sarah talk the question of salvation is raised.

> **Greta:** Do you think he'll save you?
> **Sarah:** What from?
> **Greta:** Yourself.
> **Sarah:** He has to save himself first.
> **Greta:** Does he?
> **Sarah:** We all have.
> **Greta:** Are we worth saving? (*C* 347-348)

Where once traditional Christian theology answered this question through offering an interpretation of salvation through the death and resurrection of Jesus on behalf of sinners, these characters are faced with the task of saving themselves and believing themselves worthy of salvation. Where the community was once nourished and sustained by the memory of Jesus this community gathered in the graveyard must be faithful to their own truth and their own stories.

Greta, now an orphan, searches for a myth of origins. Her parents' inadequate parenting (in a doll's house) and in particular her mother's failure to initiate her into an awareness of her sexuality leaves her feeling lost and wanting herself back, 'to be what I used to be' (*C* 350). Maela finally admits that her daughter is dead. She tells her story of her daughter's death from cancer on Bloody Sunday and her subsequent walk through the dead in the streets of Derry. The scene of her meeting with the doctor at the hospital is played with Dido as the doctor. The painful memory of the day comes back in a moving speech, which is like a vision of crucifixion or hell on earth. The sense of disorientation is huge. The devastation of her personal experience is mirrored through the streets as she hears of more and more dead. Her naming of the streets, William Street and Ferryquay Street and the Strand and Rosville Street and Great James Street stresses the particularity of place and makes what is happening almost unbearable. The memories flow into one another, fluid almost interchangeable as she allows herself to remember the pain and the horror.

> They opened fire and shot them dead. I'm not dead. Where are there dead in Derry? Let me look on the dead. Jesus, the dead. The innocent dead. There's thirteen dead in Derry. Where am I? What day is it? Sunday. Why is the sun bleeding? It's pouring blood. I want a priest. Give me a priest. Where am I? In Great James Street. It's full of chemists. I need a tonic for my nerves. For my head. For my heart. Pain in my heart. Breaking heart. I've lost one. I've lost them all. They had no hair. She had fire. She opened fire on herself. When I wasn't looking she caught cancer. It burned her. She was thirteen. It was Sunday. I have to go to Mass. I have to go to Mass. I have to go to Mass. Dido, take me to Mass Dido. (*C* 352)

As Dido questions Maela, like a quiz-master, there is a sense of an old order returning. The parameters of their world are being redefined and they may be able to inhabit it fully once more. Scene six is set on Saturday evening and finds the characters in party mood, singing football songs and remembering the old days. Teams are decided for a quiz which is a complete farce. The humour, banter and camaraderie between the players are in evidence as they enter into a new space of relationship. The transgressive space of play opens the characters to new possibilities within themselves. The truths of their lives begin to emerge. Sarah wants to have a child. Greta questions Paul about his madness and his pyramid building. He associates it with The Last Judgement and the dead rising. He feels that if they do not rise tonight that he will go and join them. He carries the war within his head, in particular the horror of Bloody Sunday. When Greta begins to rip apart his black plastic bag he stops her:

> Stop it. Stop it. (grabs the plastic bag off Greta) The plastic bags. They threw them over the dead. Bury them decently. Put them in the ground. Carrying the dead like a pile of rubbish through Derry on Bloody Sunday. Don't tear the plastic bags. Don't defile their coffin. Don't, please, don't. Don't let them die. Don't let me go mad. If they die, I'll go mad. I have to keep carrying them. That's where I keep them. Give them back to me. (C 368)

Seph says that Greta hates being herself. Seph talks about being a traitor, repeating the ritual action of tearing down the tricolour. He dissociated himself from those who wanted to avenge the dead by informing on the living. Seph, like Paul, still carries the war in his head. Hark in a similar way chose to live by not going on hunger strike. There is a sense of failed manhood about Hark (or at least failed in relation to a particular definition of manhood).

> I can't. Can't fire, can't kill, can't eat. Coward. I'm a coward. Want to eat. Want to live, I want to live. And I can't face the dead. Will the dead go away and stop haunting me? I cannot kill to avenge you. All I could have killed was myself. And I couldn't. I can't. Come back to me, Sarah, I'm dead. Come back and raise the dead. (*C* 372)

The play repudiates the notion of sacrifice that underpins the ideology of war. Whereas an ideology of sacrifice celebrates and glorifies death, Hark and Seph chose life instead. But the sense of death continues to haunt the living. Greta carries it within her, intimately within her female self. Her dirty joke is the story of her life. The dirty trick that life has played on her. When she learns that she cannot conceive she goes to her parents' grave:

> She said, Mammy, Daddy, I'm afraid. And she saw the dead. She saw herself. She saw nothing, for she is nothing. She is not a woman anymore. She's a joke. A dirty joke … (*C* 373)

Having told her story Greta confirms that the dead will rise tonight.

The intertextuality of their lives is stressed as the narratives of their broken, fractured lives give way to a shared remembering of films and poetry, from the Indians in the Western who had 'the best words...like poetry' (*C* 375) to the verses of *The Traveller*. The sense of 'phantom listeners' is heightened by the recitation of the poem in a graveyard. The poetry opens the space of ritual and deeper remembering, where forgiveness might be possible.

Paul recites the names, ages and addresses of the thirteen who were killed on Bloody Sunday. The characters' responses show a personal appropriation of traditional imagery, prayer and ritual, associated with the dead. Taken outside of the churches, it is nonetheless located in the liminal, sacred space of a graveyard. Christian imagery of death and resurrection continues to permeate their prayer. The theme of forgiveness, while not exclusively a Christian one, is still present, although equally removed from its religious setting.

> **Hark:** Perpetual light shine upon you. Rest in peace.
> **Seph:** Bloody Sunday.
> **Sarah:** Sunday.
> **Greta:** Sunday.
> **Sarah:** Sunday.
> **Greta:** Wash the dead.
> **Paul:** Sunday.
> **Maela:** Bury the dead.
> **Seph:** Sunday.
> **Sarah:** Raise the dead.
> **Hark:** Sunday.
> **Dido:** Do you see the dead?
> **Greta:** The dead beside you.
> **Maela:** The dead behind you.
> **Sarah:** The dead before you.
> **Greta:** Forgive the dead.
> **Maela:** Forgive the dying.
> **Sarah:** Forgive the living.
> **Paul:** Forgive yourself.
> **Hark:** Forgive yourself.

> **Seph:** Forgive yourself.
> **Maela:** Bury the dead.
> **Greta:** Raise the dying.
> **Sarah:** Wash the living. (*C* 378-379)

The ritual rhythm of this prayer with its repetition and call to forgiveness and hope expresses the heightened state of awareness of the characters. It echoes the ancient Christian prayer – *The Lorica*, more commonly known as *St. Patrick's Breastplate*. It offers protection in a similar manner and sees the continuity of life and death, in the enduring presence of the dead in the memories of those who survive them. Having gathered and told their stories, having faced their terrible pain, having healed their fractured memories, having shared food and drink and song and laughter they have been enabled to move through their darkness into light. Stage directions indicate that:

Light breaks through the graveyard. Birdsong begins. Light illumines them all. They listen, looking at each other, in the light. They lie down and sleep. It is now morning. Dido alone is awake in the graveyard. (C 379)

The final speech is Dido's.

> What happened? Everything happened, nothing happened, whatever you want to believe, I suppose (*C*. 379).

Was there a resurrection of the dead? Some scholars would say that Christ rose in the hearts of the believers. Through the ritual space of theatre a group of people enacted the transformation of their lives and were witnessed by others. Dido assumes almost a mythical status, world wanderer, between times, and places. The totality of the world for the duration of this play has been the city of Derry, its streets, and its graveyard. As he drops flowers on the sleepers his words are like a blessing, invoking protection, as he urges the characters to watch themselves and to remember him. His final word is 'Play', an invitation to a pace of freedom, to which the newly risen ones are now called.

1 Elie Weisel, *Night* (London: Penguin Books, 1981), p.76-77.
2 Cathy Caruth, quoting Greenberg and van der Kolk in her introduction to the second part of the book, *Trauma: Explorations in Memory*, ed. Cathy Caruth (Baltimore, Johns Hopkins University Press, 1995), p.152.
3 Riana O'Dwyer, 'Dancing in the Borderlands: The Plays of Frank McGuinness' in *The Crows behind the Plough: History and Violence in Anglo-Irish Poetry and Drama*, ed. Geert Lernout (Amsterdam, Atlanta: Rodopi, 1991), pp.99 -115, p.112.
4 Frank McGuinness, *Carthaginians* in *Plays 1* (London: Faber and Faber, 1996), p.298. All further references to the play are from this same edition and will be included in parentheses in the main body of the text.
5 Cathy Caruth, op.cit. p.5.
6 Helen Lojek, 'Difference *Without* Indifference: The Drama of Frank McGuinness and Anne Devlin', in *Eire–Ireland*, Vol. 25, 1990, pp.56–68, p.58.
7 ibid. p.68.

Directing McGuinness Plays
Sarah Pia Anderson in conversation with Sharon Braden

[**Sarah Pia Anderson** is a theatre, film, and television director currently living and working in Los Angeles. She is also a tenured professor in the Department of Theatre and Dance at the University of California, Davis. Her work in British television is extensive and includes an episode of the Emmy award winning series *Prime Suspect* (starring Helen Mirren). In the U.S. she has directed episodes of *ER*, *Nothing Sacred* (Peabody Award for series; Prism Award for Directing), *Profiler*, *Gilmore Girls*, and *Ally McBeal*. From the mid-70s through the mid-90s she worked extensively in the British theatre. She directed the world premieres of *Carthaginians* (Abbey Theatre, 1988 and Hampstead Theatre Club 1989) and *Mary and Lizzie* (RSC, 1989), as well as McGuinness's adaptations of *Rosmersholm* (Royal National Theatre and La Mama, 1987), *Hedda Gabler* (Roundabout Theatre, 1994), and *Three Sisters* (UC Davis, 1995). Anderson spoke with Sharon Braden at the University of California, Davis on 8 May 2002.]

SB: *As a director of McGuinness's work, could you tell us a little bit about your working relationship with him and how you see that?*

SPA: I've had the longest working relationship with any writer, with Frank. When we first met, I had been asked by Sir Peter Hall to direct *Rosmersholm* at the Royal National Theatre and I needed a translation of the play to be done quickly. Di Trevis was working at the National at the time and she suggested I meet Frank. Frank at that time had just won an Evening Standard Award. He was becoming well known and she said, 'Oh, you have to meet this playwright. He's brilliant and he may be able to help you with this translation.' So, thanks to Di, I met Frank, and it turned out that *Rosmersholm* was one of his most favourite plays. So much so that in his play *The Factory Girls* he had named a character after the heroine of *Rosmersholm*, Rebecca West. He said he'd be delighted to do the work and we went from there. Frank was in rehearsals at the National and in New York when the play was put on at La Mama. Frank then asked me to work with him on his next new play, *Carthaginians* – he asked me to direct *Carthaginians* – and luckily the producers at the Abbey agreed.

What is it like working with him? I think because I understand – I like the content of his work, the plays – we were just very much in sympathy – in terms of what he was wrestling with, a combination of personal and national ... I want to say guilt, though guilt comes into it, that is not the whole thing. How do you come to terms with the past? – which I think is sort of underlying a lot of his work. How important is the past? What is the past? How does it affect one in the present? I think pretty much everything I have done with Frank has been on that theme – with the exception of the Chekhov, which was another experience. The past doesn't play such a strong part in the proceedings as in Ibsen's work, but nonetheless it is there. With Chekhov it is more to do with the variety of human nature, the paradoxical nature of us human beings that we can be laughing one minute, crying the next, and then suffering, and then joy, and then somehow carry on. There was a mutual kind of fascination with the human condition in that respect. And I suppose it was more of a relationship with Chekhov, but I think that the work on Ibsen, for me, was more connected with his (Frank's) work as a playwright where these issues were just dealt with in different ways – whether it was Ireland's troubles or the struggles of a gay identity. I suppose we just coincided at a time where I understood intuitively, rather than intellectually, what he was trying to achieve.

I saw it as my job to really reveal the plays, not necessarily to edit them, not necessarily to improve upon them and I didn't have any axe to grind about Frank being a great playwright or not. The plays, for me, were a form of exploration and the fact that they were successful sometimes, not successful at other times, was not a surprise to me, nor was it even particularly relevant. Of course it is always nice to have a success, but I didn't work with Frank because I thought we would be successful. It was a journey of exploration, exhausting at times, because Frank has a big heart and a big imagination and he is demanding in lots of ways. And I don't mean as a person – he is very generous. He is very easy to work with – I found him very easy to work with in rehearsal. He was very connected to the actors and really open to changing things when they weren't working. I don't really know how many changes he ultimately made in these texts because I can't compare them any longer with the rehearsal text, but I am sure there were quite a few changes. That was exciting. It is also exciting to be doing new work – you don't quite know what it is.

SB: *I know you have been directing television, film, and stage plays for quite a while. What do you see as the major similarities and differences between film/TV and the stage?*

SPA: Well, the biggest difference really is the camera. In theatre the audience is in a seat and they have basically one point of view and the director orchestrates the action on stage to focus the text, and other elements, to communicate the story. But with television and film, with the cinematic medium, it is the camera that moves us from place to place and the audience still remains in one place but their viewpoint is being shifted for them and the director orchestrates their point of view.

There are other differences between working for the stage and the screen as a director. Obviously, the way in which a play is rehearsed and worked on is really entirely different. Film and television rely much more heavily on the actors being prepared both in terms of their characterization and also their lines. A lot of time is spent in the theatre rehearsing in order for the performance to be reproduced on a nightly basis. With film the actor never has to reproduce the performance except for the number of takes it requires to get the performance. So the whole mechanism of how you put the piece together is different. You don't have to worry about memorization so much for the actors or memorization of the movement or any of the elements. With film the director spends a lot more time in preparation than the actors would and a lot more time in post-production.

I suppose film is probably more the director's medium than the stage. In the theatre, when the actors are on stage, there is not a lot that the director is controlling, but the director has a lot more control with film and television because of the point of view. Actors on stage are responsible for focusing the audience in a way that they aren't with the camera. That is up to the cinematographer, the director, and the editor.

SB: *What do you see as the major challenges facing actors that are approaching McGuinness's work? Are there things that you think make his work difficult for actors?*

SPA: Yes there are. I'm not sure they make his work difficult, but there are challenges – like you might say that Shakespeare was difficult or Beckett was difficult. The language is not naturalistic. If you look at *Carthaginians*, the sentences are all very short and they are also quite rhythmic. They are written in such a way that if you simply read the dialogue it would create a particular rhythm – if you simply read it. But when you inhabit it, as in a performance, that rhythm gets broken. The first rhythm is Frank's rhythm. It has to get broken for the play to live. That kind of rhythm also exists in his translations of *Rosmersholm* and *Hedda Gabler* (which I have directed). He has a particular voice, but in order for the play to stand on its own as a performed piece, the actors necessarily have to break that down because their characters have to factor into that. There is also an emotional transition at every full stop. In *Carthaginians* you have a change of emotional gear every time there is a full stop. And if you don't, if an actor doesn't achieve that, then the story doesn't get told, it just becomes like a lot of short sentences. There is no real dramatic (as opposed to literary) life in the language. So there is a tension, because the actors have to honour the rhythm (Frank's), and yet ignore it. It's quite complex.

The other issue regarding *Carthaginians*, unlike a lot of other plays that I have worked on, is that the characters speak quite indirectly to each other. Occasionally directly, but you notice that whenever there is direct contact, it is generally confrontational and there is some kind of climax in the dramatic action, followed by catharsis. The meaning of what they are saying most of the time is conveyed obtusely, the way a community that knows itself very well communicates; you don't communicate directly, there is a kind of osmosis that goes on. There is an intuition at work because they just know each other so well and he (Frank) uses that in *Carthaginians* so that characters understand how each person is feeling by physical gesture as well as language. There is an intimate knowledge that the characters have of each other, but it is unspoken, and that means that in terms of acting you have to find those moments and they have to be as real as the spoken text. That is what actually makes a performance different from a reading of the play.

SB: *Some literary critics have talked about McGuinness's characters as essentially stereotypical and lacking in depth. That perhaps speaks to what you are talking about. In McGuinness's plays you have a character that lives only partially on the page. It takes the embodiment of the actor to capture all of the subtlety that he is bringing forth in the language and to make these moments of silence part of this connection and this community.*

SPA: That is really well put and accurate. Literary critics have often missed this. I have had conversations with people about it, but it is so different when you are working on the piece. The language is deceptively simple too. But it is what made working with Frank on Ibsen so good, because Norwegian and Swedish are not full of qualifying adverbs and adjectives. They are not like English. They are much more like a Germanic language where the repetition of words gives them their emphasis. Now when you look at that language, literally translated onto the page, it is just repetition. But when you imagine that every time a person repeats a word they say it slightly differently, by the time you've got to the end of the list, that word has a more layered and therefore deeper meaning.

SB: *That reminds me of* Observe the Sons of Ulster *and dancing ... 'dance in the temple of the Lord'* ...

SPA: Yes, and it is a theme with Frank, the way he uses language like a drum beat. That was very effective, I think, in his translation of *Rosmersholm*, which is so much about not being able to free oneself from the past. And repetition in a way. The theme of the play, and the way that Ibsen wrote. He (Ibsen) did not make things clear when people opened their mouths. It was not as clear as some of these English translations would have us believe. They try to make Ibsen less obtuse. *Hedda Gabler* is a perfect example of that. It is an impenetrable play in its original language. It is so difficult to understand what Ibsen was actually talking about with Hedda – what actually happened in her past, what went on with Lovborg. And it is deliberate. It is deliberate and it remains a mystery.

SB: *So do you think then that McGuinness's translation of* Hedda *works on adding that deeper meaning back in terms of repetition, etc.?*

SPA: Yes. He just refuses to go to the full use of English in the sense that literary criticism might wish him to. He uses words sparingly and repeats them in the same way as Ibsen, and curiously it creates a mystery, though the actual language is simpler. So if you are reading it, it could look banal, but when you are working with the actual text, and the subtext, it is not banal at all. It is just a very economic form of expression. It is economic, that is the word. And I think that is what is true of aspects of *Mary and Lizzie*, but particularly *Carthaginians*. It is incredibly economic.

SB: *I thought I would move on to your directing experience with a wide array of audiences. I know that you have directed in the United States, Britain, and Ireland. Perhaps you could speak to how audiences in different places seem to receive McGuinness's work?*

SPA: That is really hard to answer because I'm not sure that I'm that aware of how differently the audiences respond. As far as Frank's work goes, I really had one experience of a piece of his work being put in front of two different types of audiences and that was with *Carthaginians*. It opened in the Abbey during the Dublin Theatre Festival and then was subsequently produced, the same production but with cast changes, at the Hampstead Theatre Club. And so there was one with an intensely Irish audience, presented in Frank's hometown and the other was London, a more anonymous environment.

The difference I noticed was that the Irish (both in Dublin and London), really enjoyed the humour, really enjoyed the black humour and the comedy, and they understood the way that he (Frank) uses comedy – in a cathartic way. The comedy in *Carthaginians* actually heals the people who have been traumatized by the terrible events in Derry on Bloody Sunday.

When it came to London, the cast was changed, with the exception of the actor playing Dido, but it was essentially the same set and the same production. The English audiences talked more about the play being poetic and the comedy – the humour – was not so apparent to them. It was also a time in London when Ireland was synonymous with IRA and RUC – the terrorist threats, the train station bombings. And I think that there was a kind of emotional response to the fact that the play was on and it was Irish and it was a difficult time to be confronting these issues. So it was hard to separate what was a cultural response to the actual period that we were living through and what was a real response to the play.

The Irish audiences (in Dublin) were very much involved with the play as their story, their people, their writer, their theatre. The English response was cooler. And actually more extreme in the way that people either really loved it or they just didn't get it or they didn't like it. Those are the responses I remember anyway.

SB: *Why do you think that there aren't as many U.S. productions of McGuinness's work as we might anticipate?*

SPA: I think that, generally, Americans want the mystery solved. It is a young nation, and it is the tendency of youth to want that. I identify with that need. I identify with that, 'What does it mean? What does it mean?', but Frank and I come from a culture (whether it is Irish, English, Scottish, British, whatever it is) that is not always concerned with solving that problem for the public or the audience. That is not the point. The point is to reveal the complexity. And I think that is something that is tough for people to really sit with. And increasingly so.

Another factor is Frank's use of symbolism (like you can see in *Mary and Lizzie*). It can look awkward on the page. When it is enacted it takes on a different kind of life and again it is hard to talk about, hard to describe, but there was something very ritualistic both in *Mary and Lizzie* and *Carthaginians* – the way the objects moved around the stage, which when you read it, you might go, 'Well, how is that going to work?' you know, somebody cutting their stomach open with a bayonet and a box coming out of it or in *Carthaginians* where there is a pyramid made of garbage. But what people don't understand is that these are magical elements and the theatre is a magical place and it is very hard to describe magic. Every time the play is done, that particular set of designers, director, actors will come up with different solutions. But there will remain moments of mystery and magic. And because Frank dares to do things like that I think he can sometimes be unfairly criticized and perhaps not as widely produced.

SB: *And I suppose the point is that there isn't an easy answer to these questions. His plays force the members of the audience to work through the issues themselves and to come to their own series of conclusions rather than letting them sit in the dark and just absorb someone else's answers.*

SPA: Yes, and also there is the cathartic element – in that everything that he does is about connection, community, sharing, and the seeking of redemption. It is not a bleak message: Frank's work is very entertaining. It is very funny and very moving in simple ways. So you do make the connection to it, but he is not prepared to then make it easy for people. But even Arthur Miller has complained about the way he's received by the critics in America. It is a tough place. It is a tough place to be a playwright.

SB: *McGuinness doesn't fit into any category, which I think makes people want to try to place him somewhere and then are continually frustrated by the fact that they can't....*

SPA: But I think that is just a sign of how good he is and how enduring his work will be. It still hasn't been absorbed, it hasn't been completely understood. Well, I think it is understood, but it defies an easy kind of genre definition. But again, this whole thing of magic, symbolism, and the emblematic life of the play just doesn't come off of the page in the way that it does on the stage.

Very often, people will look at the play and they'll be frustrated and want to turn it into something else because it doesn't quite fit a pre-conceived notion. I've always been more interested in things that don't quite fit because I think that they may have something new and challenging to contribute. So, again, that played into my relationship with Frank. I perceived Frank as being different and having a new voice, an interesting voice, and that was exciting to me. I am just much more interested in things that are not so identifiable – discovering their meanings. Playwrights at various times have suffered from not being understood and then have been understood and discarded. It is a cultural thing. It is what people decide at the time.

SB: *Do you think that literary criticism or textual analysis in some ways misses the point in terms of plays? I'm struggling with this a lot as I'm reading literary analyses of texts and coming from both a theatrical background and a literary background. Do you find that there is a tendency (especially with playwrights like McGuinness who think in terms of the stage rather than the page) for literary critics to miss a lot?*

SPA: I have a degree in English literature and it was always frustrating to me that we would study plays, but no one would ever talk about how they were performed. That was almost something you didn't dare to talk about, this other life. And that was years ago, back in the early 70s and I was involved in the theatre at the University and I always felt like I was doing something slightly taboo in relation to my degree. Of course, I made that taboo my life and the other part just kind of dwindled, the scholarly aspect of it. I don't think it misses the point, I just don't think it gets the whole point by any means. Similarly, I think that people who eschew literary criticism are missing the point as well. It is like looking at a painting and analyzing it, but somehow not taking into consideration how the painting is received by maybe thousands of millions of people that see it. The context of it. Where is it placed? In what time? But those who think that literary analysis of plays is all there is play into something that I really find quite disturbing generally in the arts; which is that it is fine to study the text, but let's not bother with those messy people, the artists, who actually made this text. Frank wrote *Mary and Lizzie* based on a workshop that was put together by a group of people. He may have written that play in a different way without us, but we contributed to it and the performance of it is part of its life. To simply take the text and to deny the rest of it is ludicrous.

SB: *Let's talk about* Mary and Lizzie, *which you directed in 1989 for the RSC at the Barbican.*

SPA: Yes, in The Pit.

SB: *And that was with an English cast?*

SPA: Definitely a cast that was assembled in England.

SB: *You had workshopped this script beforehand with the RSC. Can you tell us about the experience of workshopping it?*

SPA: The workshop was set up for a period of time in Stratford. Frank and I worked with the actors and basically it was a research group. We looked at material that Frank gave us. The basic story we knew. Frank wanted to tell a story about Mary and Lizzie Burns who lived with Engels, so we would read around that whole subject. Well that of course includes Marx, Engels, Freud, the Famine (the Irish Famine), understanding Irish politics, the Church, Anglicanism, and Protestantism. Well, the Anglican Church and what happened to the Catholic Church in Ireland.

So it was a lot of reading of material and then, as far as I remember, we improvised scenes. Frank would also write scenes, and he would give people tasks that he wanted them to fulfill and then they would come back to the rehearsal room and present the group with their findings. I remember once we looked at Victorian theatre, the Music Hall, and what part did that play in the life of the newly industrialized British nation. It was like a cultural study of that time period. And none of us really had any notion of what he was going to write and how he was going to put it together. It was a kind of enacted history lesson with us all throwing in our emotional responses to the subject matter. And ultimately the story, of course, is about betrayal. And I think it was quite surprising for us all to learn about the Irish Famine. I don't think any of us really knew how devastating that had been for Ireland. So we did come out of it feeling better informed about the relationship between England and Ireland, as triggered by those dreadful years of famine.

SB: *So, when you directed it at the Barbican, how was that experience different than the workshop?*

SPA: Well, it was very different because even though it had come from a workshop that we had all been so closely involved in, when we read the play, there was a good deal of amazement that this could have arisen from what we had been doing. Because what we were doing was quite realistic in many ways and the play certainly wasn't. And so, I suppose, I partly expected Frank to write an epic play of some kind. A lot of small, more realistic scenes that covered a period of time. But no.

When we looked at the first scene, the women living in the trees, it was very exciting because it was challenging to figure out 'How are we going to do this?' Especially so because the Pit at the Barbican had a low ceiling so there was no possibility of hanging people high up above the audience. And although it is a bigger space than the Peacock or Hampstead Theatre Club it was still a studio space. Philosophically and intellectually Frank was trying (within these relatively short scenes) to cover an enormous amount of ground in terms of characterization and plot. I was just amazed and delighted by the ambition of it really. Reading it again, I feel the same way. It is not quite a finished piece of work in that it is not entirely cohesive, but it does have many moments of blinding brilliance that the critics missed at the time for sure. It's a dream play.

SB: *You mentioned the Music Hall as a part of the research. Music obviously plays a big part in this play. How do you see it figuring in terms of the themes?*

SPA: I'm trying to remember when the whole notion of the music came in. I think that it was there from the beginning, that Frank wanted to use music and not just music, but have it lyrically embedded in the text. Shaun's music was very haunting.[1] It was quite romantic. It was full of longing. It actually had a very powerful emotional effect, whereas you can imagine that some of the text did not have such a simple emotional appeal.

SB: *It is a bit Brechtian.*

SPA: Yes, well, Brechtian in the sense that the play challenged the audience not to sympathize with some of the characters. And boiling that theory of alienation down – the character of the priest for example, the son who has become both Protestant and Catholic, is definitely more Brechtian in concept. But you might also have encountered him in one of Ibsen's early sagas – *Peer Gynt*, for example. Which Frank has also translated.

And then you've got this music, which was clearly asking you to go with it emotionally, and quite shamelessly manipulating the audience I think. It carried the heartbeat, if you like, of *Mary and Lizzie*, and the Irish nation. Not only was it composed by an Irishman, but the lyrics were in Irish and some of the music was based on Irish folksongs. It literally carried the theme of Ireland and *Mary and Lizzie* intertwined: betrayal, heartbreak and survival.

SB: *How did you manage to solve the living in trees?*

SPA: I think that for the living in trees Ultz [the designer] and I experimented with a system of ropes that we hung from the grid in the theatre and the women clung onto the ropes and there was a whole choreography that went on. Again, it was emblematically resolved. There weren't any trees and there was hardly any scenery.

The major scenic statement was that the set was made up of the lids of coffins. This was the stage floor. So, for example, when *Mary and Lizzie* entered the earth, one of the lids opened, a light came up and they descended into the earth that way. We took images from all over the place. It wasn't necessarily historical – literally historical. It wasn't all the same time period. The camps were Soviet labour camps; but that was because at that point the play went into the future, but there were still elements of the women in the trees in those camps as well. It was anachronistic.

I think that if we'd had a little more time and more resources we would have done even stranger things with the design. I think it is a little bit like Strindberg (Strindberg's *Dream Play*), you can do it one of several ways: you can do it with nothing or you can make the thing into a spectacle. I think that we were sort of half way between the two because it was a studio production at the RSC, so it was hard to think of it in a spectacular way. And ultimately I don't know that the play would have been best supported by that approach, but I can see how it could be done in that way.

We were also concerned with irony and comedy in the play. In the Feast of Famine it was Ultz's idea to have the women come on in huge skirts that they just spread out around them so it gave you the feeling of opulence. And of course what they were doing was singing and they were telling you the terrible story of the Irish Famine, which was truly terrible, of suffering and distress, and they looked so beautiful because, of course, they were now in heaven. When you read Frank's plays on the page (I'm trying to make sense of why people are critical of the poetry), it almost seems as though the physicalization is over-emphatic, but when they're staged and embodied, it's so different.

SB: *Could you tell us about the space for* Carthaginians? *It was a small space. It was originally done at the Peacock, correct? And a relatively small cast? How do you think that the intimacy of the space and the small cast affected the way that you directed the production?*

SPA: I think that what I decided fairly early on in the discussions with the designer (Wendy Shea) was that we would set the play on a slope on a mound. Frank really was interested in the idea of this being a burial mound. We took a trip to one of the local Neolithic sites –I think that we might even have gone to Knowth. I was very struck by the way that there were these tunnels that you go through and then there is a small piece of light. To enter the mound you go through it. When you go into the centre, you are not quite sure where you are going and then there is light. This struck me. And you do get the sense of going into the earth. And what we decided was that we were going to try to create this effect in the Peacock.

So that the design was sort of environmental, almost. The designer painted texture onto the side walls of the theatre, which made it look like the layers of the earth. You got that sense that you were in the tunnel of a burial mound. The actors sat on a rake on the stage at the end of this tunnel. It was really like a desert, I didn't want it to be green or to have that earthy, 'browny' texture, because I wanted it to remind us more of the settings of Beckett's plays or plays where there is a landscape that is not naturalistic, but creates a sense of limbo. Which is where I think the characters in *Carthaginians* find themselves. And this play is also specifically limbo because it is about members of a Catholic community, somewhere between heaven and hell.

The Peacock, of course, goes slightly down towards its stage. The seats kind of descend and then rising from the stage we had this mound. So what that meant was that this small cast, once they had taken up their positions on this stage, couldn't really move around easily because they were on a rake. There was limited movement, which I found to be essential for the way I conceived of it.

The actors were resistant at times. I don't know how they felt in the end. It is not comfortable for actors to work on a rake. They generally feel very limited by it. But I think that it worked for the play. It focused the audience's attention on the individual characters and the language and any interaction that they made became even more significant. Any physical gesture (whether it was an entrance or an exit, or the building of a pyramid, or Maela laying out her daughter's clothes), all of these gestures were heightened because their movement was limited. In the same way as with any of Beckett's plays – he traps the actors. I wasn't conscious of doing that, but I realize in hindsight that it was an unconscious kind of take on the play.

SB: *I was interested in what you just mentioned about being in limbo, in-between heaven and hell in the Catholic community. How do you see Dido fitting in that scenario?*

SPA: Dido is an outsider amongst outsiders. Dido is part of that group because all of them, in their way, are suffering from self-destructive tendencies as a result of the traumas they have been through. Well, he is part of it and he isn't. Dido, in a way, though, is a catalyst for the catharsis, because he is the link – in a sense he is like the traditional fool in any drama – he is the link between the audience and the real world outside of this artificial community that has been created within a community. He comes and goes and he brings supplies (and although Frank doesn't do this) in another play one could imagine this character would talk directly to the audience. He is more from a *commedia* tradition.

He leaves at the end of the play, and perhaps that is one of the most hopeful things. He is also the youngest person. He is not the same generation as this group of people. He is younger and he is learning from them, but ultimately he leaves. I don't know that he is so much trapped in that limbo emotionally, but I do think that he is attracted to it. They are all outsiders, but he does not experience the same shame, and the same guilt as the others. Which is why he is able to help to release them. There is definitely a way in which the character operates both inside and outside of the group, which allows for them to connect with each other and for him to leave.

SB: *Is that how you see the play within a play operating?*

SPA: *The Burning Balaclava.* Well, you know, that play is operating on at least two levels. One, of course, is just a straight parody of so many plays that were written at the time about the

Irish Troubles in the North. So it is Frank being wicked about his fellow playwrights. And also, because he is such a good playwright, it does serve that same function of facing the group with a stereotype that they are perhaps even unconsciously fulfilling in some way. I remember that when we first started working on *The Burning Balaclava*, Frank was saying that there were really specific reasons why Dido made Hark the mother, for example. The gender bending, the role reversal, was very deliberate on Dido's part. So I suppose that it is a therapeutic session that he sets up for them – which in typical fashion they eschew and reject. But somehow it works nonetheless despite themselves.

I think there is another thing about the physical aspect of this, if you can imagine it. The characters in *Carthaginians* are isolated on the stage at different points for most of the play. So it really did make the point that, although this was a group of people, they were not often physically connected. So that whenever the playwright required them to be connected, like in *The Burning Balaclava* or the quiz show, these moments of community and theatricality were highlighted. Whereas if the stage space had been much freer, the delineation between their separateness, and when they were a community would not have been so poignant.

SB: *All of the characters are there for very different reasons and come from very different backgrounds within that community...*

SPA: There is a collective, which is the group, and then there are the individuals within it who are fighting to separate. And that, I think, is the tension in the play that even though these people come from very different backgrounds, they are still Catholics in Derry and that actually characterizes them as a community. It is hard for people to understand who have not been brought up in a place where their faith has defined them both politically and spiritually, that it is very, very defining and yet each individual is wrestling within that collective to come to terms with their own sense of what it means, their own sense of guilt, and their own sense of betrayal. And so, when you are acting in the play, those are the tensions that are going on, and they are in the language, and that is why one person will say a word and another person will pick it up, and then incorporate it into their next speech. They throw the language between each other in a way that they would throw feelings. Most of what I was doing as the director was looking for the reality, looking for a very contemporary reality in it. Then to a certain extent, you let the language do its own work.

Rereading *Carthaginians*, I still think it is a very funny, very moving play. It would be a mistake to do the play entirely naturalistically, and a mistake to do it as though it was a poetic drama. Somewhere in the middle is where it sits, but you have to hold the line because the temptation to go one way or the other is always there.

SB: *The questions that keep being asked are 'So what happened?' 'So what happened?' 'Did the dead rise?' What would your response be to that?*

SPA: 'Everything happened, nothing happened.' [As Dido says at the end.] If the play's worked, you get the sense that yes, they rose, the point is *they* (the characters we've been watching on stage all night) rose, *they're* the dead, *they* rose. As a group, they brought themselves back to life on earth. They brought themselves back to themselves. There was no *Deus ex Machina*. And if you are waiting for the poltergeist to appear or expecting it to be like a murder mystery, then it's just not going to happen. It is also as I said; Frank is not prepared to solve the mystery. What is the point of doing a play, what is the point of putting something in front of people of this kind of complexity, if you have an easy answer for them? Where would be the fun in that?

---

[1] Shaun Davey composed the music for *Mary and Lizzie* and for McGuinness's later play *Mutabilitie*.

Watching Over Frank McGuinness's Stereotypes*
Helen Lojek

The opening of Frank McGuinness's *Someone Who'll Watch Over Me* at New York's Booth Theatre in November 1992, following successful runs at London's Hampstead and Vaudeville theatres, provided the first opportunity for major American audiences to encounter the work of a playwright who has been a significant force in Irish theatre at least since his 1986 *Observe the Sons of Ulster Marching Towards the Somme*. Winner of such accolades as the London Standard Award, the Rooney Prize for Irish Literature, the London Fringe Award, and the Harvey's Best Play Award, McGuinness has exhibited a restless creativity in works ranging from the straight realism of *The Factory Girls* (1982) to the extravagant experimentation and expressionism of *Innocence* (1986). In *Someone Who'll Watch Over Me*, he blends elements from both extremes (and his first American character) to create what is for American audiences his most accessible play yet. And with it he has added a New York Drama Critics Circle Award to his list of prizes.

In this play about Middle East hostages such familiar elements as stereotypes, clichés, pop culture, and literary quotations provide refreshingly new perspectives, and without ever focusing specifically on the current Irish 'Troubles' McGuinness casts a revealing light on the human factors which lie

*This article first appeared in Modern Drama *38 (1995) pp.348-361.*

behind both those Troubles and the Middle East crisis. Most amazingly, he discovers behind depressing current newspaper headlines stories that renew our faith in the power of the human spirit. The back cover of the published text sets the play's basic situation: 'An Englishman, an Irishman and an American are locked up together in a cell in the Middle East.'[1] New York playgoers got comparable information from the program: 'a lowbrow Irish journalist' is 'chained to the wall of [a] dingy Beirut basement along with an athletic American and a prissy Brit.'[2] For audience members who have read neither text nor program and have missed the implications of the characters' sharply contrasting accents, Edward (the Irish journalist) provides his own formulaic summary: 'There were three bollocks in a cell in Lebanon. An Englishman, an Irishman, and an American' (17).

Wherever and however the formulation is phrased, it sets a familiar context, that of the international ethnic joke, which begins in the same conventional terms. 'Two Englishmen, two Germans, and two Americans were on a ship that sank,' the cocktail wit starts his tale. Or, 'An Englishman, a Frenchman, and a Texan are on an overloaded plane about to crash. ...' Such jokes depend on a common set of regional stereotypes – stereotypes that they in turn popularize and circulate. Like ethnic nicknames, the jokes can be forms of verbal aggression, and such humour relies on stereotypes that are generally regarded as contributing factors in the deep-seated prejudices that pit groups against each other.[3]

McGuinness's characters provide an abundance of that delight in the familiar that is basic to ethnic jokes. The American is physical, competitive, concerned with commercial value (in this case, his own value to his captors), proud of his Americanism, concerned with his looks. In the play's first productions (in London and New York), Adam was cast as an African American. His own testimony that he also possesses an unusually large penis thus had an additional ring of stereotype.[4]

The Irishman is Catholic, likes soccer, horses, and drink, has a wife to whom he is unfaithful and children to whom he is an absentee father. He also has the gift of gab. And (by his own testimony) he shares the belief that the Irish invented foreplay – and that drink is foreplay (9). In fact, on the surface this Irishman epitomizes the very qualities of 'easy buffoonery and sentiment' which W.B. Yeats, Lady Gregory, and Edward Martyn sought to banish from the Irish stage. The Englishman is precise, prissy, educated, attached to his mother, and worried others will question his sexuality. He regards Irish as a dialect of English and cannot understand why he is being blamed for a famine that took place one hundred and fifty years ago. Names underscore these ethnic stereotypes. Adam Canning is the American. Edward Sheridan has (as Dr. Johnson said of Thomas Sheridan) 'the disadvantage of being an Irishman.' He also has playwright Richard Brinsley Sheridan's ability to mock English affectations and national pride. The Englishman is Michael Watters – a name that allows the Irishman to inquire politely, 'Do you mind me calling you Mick?' (10).

The three cope with captivity in predictable ways: the American Adam exercises; the Irish Edward escapes into imagination and verbal wit; the English Michael remembers the lessons of World War II and keeps a stiff upper lip. Such national differences are underlined and reinforced by the radically different accents with which the three characters speak, and since they are the play's *only* three characters the differences remain clear and sharp.

These stereotypes emerge in the context of a rollicking humour that is, in Edward's words, 'how we get by' (10). Generally the stereotypes are not imposed on one character by another but shared by all: the Englishman is as proud and certain of his stiff upper lip as the others are amused and certain of it; the Irishman himself first mocks the religious divisions characteristic of his country; and it is the American who mentions (with both pride and humour) his nation's obsession with commercial value. Such antic exaggerations are part of the sometimes desperate humour in which the prisoners join – pitting play and laughter and boisterous creativity against despair. They are also part of a process Seamus Deane has described (in a discussion which focuses largely on the English and the Irish) as typical of stereotyping in a colonial environment. Stereotypes are 'mutually generative,' he suggests. The 'community that exercises power' stereotypes not just the Other, but also itself, and both groups internalize the stereotypes. Part of the process of liberation from the stereotypes involves taking 'possession' of them and converting them into renovated, empowering images.[5]

In Edward and Michael, the Irishman and the Englishman, McGuinness has created characters who have taken possession of their stereotypes and are no longer bound by them. Adam, at least to this American viewer, is more problematic. The stereotype is recognizable and certainly as accurate as the other ethnic stereotypes. Somehow, though, McGuinness is not so successful in finding his way through the American stereotype to the human beneath. Perhaps because McGuinness himself is less familiar with the United States than with Ireland and England, Adam has not taken sufficient possession of his stereotype. The fact that Adam is often portrayed as an African American probably adds to McGuinness's difficulties, and Adam remains too exclusively Other to be as satisfactory a use of stereotype as are Michael and Edward. Ironically, then, despite the horror of Adam's off-stage death, and the agony it yields for the surviving prisoners (especially Edward), the second act, with its simpler interplay between more successfully realized stereotypes, is somehow easier. In general, though, the play – like the characters – moves quickly beyond the limits of stereotype.

The hostages need no social psychologist to remind them of the further truth that stereotypes are not always negative and do not always lead to prejudice or discrimination, especially on an individual level:[6] the group that develops within the cell, the society which they build and share, is a practical lesson in such truths. Though full of clichés about their own and other ethnic groups and fond of having a bit of fun with the stereotypes, these men do not, for the most part, indulge in prejudice or discrimination against each other. Common sense suggests this lack of discrimination results not just from the physical separation insured by the chains holding them to the wall but also from the in-group solidarity bred by the out-group hostility of the Arab captors.[7]

These prisoners must depend on each other, both for the preservation of their physical well-being and for the preservation of their emotional/psychological well-being. Initially they may have used ethnic jokes as the outside world uses them – to jockey among themselves for status and power. Gradually, however, they stop slagging each other and unite against their captors. Ironically, the shared outlook that unites them depends in part on their use of stereotypes (stereotypes of the very sort they have stopped hurling at each other) to distinguish themselves from their captors. They form, in fact, their own group, and like other groups they develop social cohesion and order by developing a general (and transmittable) set of values.[8]

As soon as Michael joins Adam and Edward in captivity, the 'experienced' hostages begin teaching the newcomer the set of values they have established with which to meet the out-group of captors (who never appear on stage). When Michael sobs and pleads for release, for example, Adam reprimands him quickly and sharply.

> You mustn't let them hear you cry. They're listening to you as you speak. They want you to weep. Don't ever do that in here. I'm warning you, don't weep. That's what they want. So don't cry. Laugh. Do you hear me? Laugh. ... Laugh, damn you. (11)

The laughter which has helped them to deal with adversity – to 'get by' – here becomes a weapon in the fight to protect themselves from the captors, who are demarcated by their exclusion from the laughter and by the generalization that all the captors delight in tears from the captives. Michael learns this lesson so well that at the end of the play, after Adam's presumed death, when it is Edward who is near emotional collapse, he can give the lesson back.

> Laugh, Edward ... They can hear you crying. Laugh ... Laugh, you bastard, laugh ... Laugh. (56)

Examples of parallel socialization processes abound. When the play opens Adam is insisting Edward do push-ups, anticipating the competitions they can have once Edward is in shape. After Adam's death, it is Edward who urges Michael to get in shape, and he too promises future competitions. Adam and Edward also teach Michael how to describe his life as though it were a movie, and in a scene reminiscent of *The Kiss of the Spider Woman* the prisoners entertain each other with rollicking film parodies. The American builds on Sam Peckinpah's model (with overtones of *The Sound of Music* and perhaps of *Suddenly, Last Summer* as well); the Englishman steals images from Richard Attenborough; and the Irishman creates a scenario which the others recognize as Irish – presumably because of its resemblance to *My Left Foot* – but whose director they cannot name. They also write imaginary letters home, share imaginary drinks, and re-create real sporting events (including the 1977 Wimbledon Ladies' Tennis Final, after which Irish Edward in his role of Queen Elizabeth asks Virginia Wade what she does and declares a fondness for the smell of sweat).

At first Adam and Edward use these antic games to entertain the newly arrived Michael. Essentially, they are the performers and he the spectator. Though initially confused by their play, Michael soon shares their delight and joins as a full participant. A link has been established; the in-group of two has become three. In fact, the major survival technique for these prisoners is the forging of just such links so that they become a group with shared experiences – movies, letters, callisthenics, music, laughter, and admitted fears. In a sense, they are creating their own folklore, and – like all folklores – it is a bricolage of snippets from remembered reading, viewing, and experience.

This group of three functions in opposition to the dangerous out-group of Arab captors, and the three are well aware of their dependence on each other. After an emotional outburst, for example, Michael says, 'I apologize for that dreadful outburst. I may have put us all at risk by that dreadful outburst' (32).

At one point, however, the prisoners fantasize about inviting their captives to the imaginary drinking party they are having.

> **Edward:** They've heard us enjoying ourselves. ... They don't approve of this ... What are we going to do? ... We haven't done as we're told. We've got them in a state of shock. ... Will I drown them with drink? Will I drown them? ... will we let them sit down? Will we make space for them? Do you in-

vite them to the party? ... Take the weight off your feet boys. Imagine it's a wedding ... Bit of a song. A story. The same the world over. Have a drink if you like. We won't tell. Join us. (34-35)

While it reminds us of how different the world would be if we all drank and sang together, however, Edward's fantasy remains unrealized, and for the most part the captives – having forged from their own separate nationalities a survivors' group – are content to stereotype the out-group of captors with whom they must deal. The stereotype itself becomes an essential part of their definition of the Arabs as 'Other'. The Arabs are omnipresent, ever watchful, delighted by signs of weakness, irrational, and 'excitable' because 'The sand blows up their skirts and they're not allowed to scratch themselves' (4). 'Who are they?' asks Michael. 'The enemy,' replies Edward (12), and that is all they need to know.

It is not, however, all they *do* know, and their very willingness to imagine a joint banquet is a significant delineator between them and their captors. These ethnic representatives have learned not only how to tolerate their own differences and discover their mutual humanity, but also how to point parallels between the Bible and the Koran and how to imagine a wider banquet attended by people with non-adversarial differences. In the cell's atmosphere of tolerance, the cultural differences among the captives emerge not as mutually antagonistic, but as mutually enriching. They can at least imagine extending such tolerance to and gaining such enrichment from the Arabs. Adam expands on his reading from the Koran, for example, to emphasize an inclusive human community which begins in his large family of foster children and extends outward: 'Forgive me, my sisters and my brothers, for doubting if you were sisters and brothers. Forgive me, my foes, for calling you my foes. In your good book lies the way to power and to peace' (23). And he notes the Koran's apparent acceptance of other religions: 'to you, your religion, and to me my religion' (27). He also notes the negative commonalities that link captives and captors: 'Arab? English Arab? Irish Arab? Right, guys? Jesus, these guys don't need to tear us apart. We can tear each other apart' (25).

That said, there is an unsettling extent to which the Arab captors in this play are caricatures of the sort so eloquently analyzed by Edward Said in *Covering Islam* and *Cultural Imperialism*. At one point Michael says an Arab has wept, apparently in reaction to the killing of Adam, but it is an isolated instance of Arab individuality. Always off-stage, the Arabs are determining influences in the captives' lives, and for the most part they are anonymous and uniform. No suspicion that they may have reasons for their actions – or even that they may exhibit individual differences as profound as those which divide the captives – clouds our impression of them as uniform, anonymous Other. And that Other is in a threateningly 'confrontational relationship with whatever is normal, Western, everyday, "ours"'.[9] Like an illustration for Said's analysis, McGuinness's play presents captives who are like us and therefore seem 'normal', and captors we can never know directly and who therefore seem abnormal. Such divisions seem likely to persist unless an invasion from outer space encourages humans to unite against an even larger group of hostile Others – or unless, following Julia Kristeva's suggestion, 'By recognizing [the stranger] within ourselves, we are spared detesting him in himself.'[10] Without such recognition, situations like the one in this play seem fated to recur.

In crafting this play, which is dedicated 'Do Bhrian Fear Cróga' ('To Brian, a Brave Man'), McGuinness clearly had in mind the situation of his fellow Irishman Brian Keenan. Keenan was abducted from his teaching post at American University Beirut and spent over four years in captivity – most of it in the company of English journalist John McCarthy, much of it in close proximity to three American hostages, and three years of it chained to a wall. Keenan's moving account of his experience, *An Evil Cradling* (published about two months after McGuinness's play appeared), includes a poem by McGuinness, and McGuinness reviewed the book for the *The Irish Times*. In Keenan's book there actually is a joint meal – a birthday celebration for one prisoner arranged by the captors. Given the deliberate cruelty of these same captors and their continued imprisonment of the Westerners, however, the semblance of fellowship becomes a cruel parody of what genuine tolerance might produce. In other ways as well, Keenan's description of captivity closely parallels McGuinness's, confirming the accuracy (if that is an issue) of McGuinness's sense that humour, memory, competition, and linguistic flights of fancy may become means of staving off the horrors of confinement and deprivation.

In a press conference soon after his release, Keenan clenched his hand to demonstrate the similarity of a fist and a hand holding a pen or paintbrush. 'With the creative hand', he suggested, 'people could contain, overcome and conquer the fist.'[11] The creativity of the men in Keenan's real cell and the men in McGuinness's stage cell helped them conquer the fists of their captors. If we are lucky the creativity of Keenan and McGuinness will help us all conquer fists.

Keenan makes explicit a parallel that in a somewhat more muted form also informs McGuinness's play. 'I, who grew up in Belfast', Keenan explains, 'perhaps knew the terrorist mind better than any other hostage.'[12] With knowledge comes a degree of power, and Keenan adopts techniques of resistance that have a special resonance for the Irish – the hunger strike and going 'on the blanket' (refusing to wear prison clothing). Keenan's use of such procedures reminds us of the difficulty of defining Irish identity. A Belfast Protestant, he was travelling on a green (Irish Republic) passport and used techniques of resistance most recently associated with Belfast nationalists (most of whom are Catholic). The fact that many Belfast Protestants perceived Keenan as a nationalist complicated efforts to work for his release. The Arabs, of course, are uninterested in such fine distinctions. In both play and reality they are unimpressed by the green passport of neutrality. They see these English-speaking Occidentals as the uniform, anonymous, and threatening Other that the Arabs seem to the captives. Edward's frustrated bewilderment at the Arabs' inability to distinguish him from British and American imperialists is ironic in juxtaposition to the mask of uniformity that is his view of them.

Irish authors can never entirely avoid questions, suggestions, and insistences about the relation of their works to contemporary Irish realities. In other plays McGuinness addresses such issues through the distancing devices of history (*Observe the Sons of Ulster Marching Towards the Somme*, 1986) or through antic mixtures of myth, fantasy, and farce (*Carthaginians*, 1988). In *Someone Who'll Watch Over Me* the Belfast/Beirut parallels of imprisonment, terrorism, and torture are so much a part of the material itself that they need little direct mention. While Edward and Michael raise the old issues of language and exploitation and Famine, then, there is no need to be explicit about the relation of these issues to the present situation. More direct and unavoidable parallels come when Edward responds to Adam's death with a hunger strike (39); and when he and Michael adopt a Derry woman's summary of her city's troubles ('Ridiculous') as the only possible summary of their own situation (46). 'I've seen it at home before', Edward says of religious intolerance (27). 'I leave one kip at home to come to this kip here' (3). Echoing a wartime poster slogan, Edward also points to the understanding in both Beirut and Belfast that 'Careless talk costs lives' (36). Keenan, like Seamus Heaney in *North*, chooses the more paradoxical phrase, 'Whatever you say say nothing.'[13]

A litany of Irish place names runs throughout the play, and Edward's ritualistic chanting of the station stops from Howth to Booterstown is reminiscent of the chanted place names McGuinness included in *Observe the Sons of Ulster*. Such use of place names is not unique to McGuinness's plays but runs through works by Irish writers as diverse as (among others) Brian Friel, Anne Devlin, and Jennifer Johnston. Seamus Heaney's reminder that the ancient Irish genre of *dinnseanchas* produced poems and tales 'which relate the original meanings of place names and constitute a form of mythological etymology'[14] helps establish the lineage of this ritualistic use of place names. Seamus Deane, in a context of colonialism and post-colonialism, discusses 'Field Day's preoccupation with naming' and characterizes naming as 'an act of possession'.[15] Edward Said identifies the 'cartographic' impulse of anti-imperialism, through which the colonized seek to reclaim their geography from the colonizers, and reminds us that the 1916 proclamation of Irish independence asserted 'the right of the people of Ireland to the ownership of Ireland'.¹⁶ The critical contexts set by Heaney, Deane, and Said clarify the extent to which there is much Irish form as well as content in this play about the Middle East.

Parallels between Ireland and the Middle East reinforce the play's examination of stereotypes in important ways. The private sphere of three captives merges into the public sphere of political unrest and terrorism, and Beirut merges with Belfast. We join three individual hostages in discovering commonalities beneath (or above) their differences. Simultaneously, we discover commonalities beneath varying regional differences. Though not all of these commonalities are positive, they reveal what links us as humans and raise the possibility that, in Keenan's words, 'in the most inhuman of circumstances men grow and deepen in humanity' (xiii).

McGuinness, in his review of Keenan's book, discusses types and tolerance in terms that are at least as pertinent to *Someone Who'll Watch Over Me* as they are to *An Evil Cradling*.

> Keenan frequently attributes his survival to his Irishness, but he is decidedly untypical, as an Irish *man* in particular, in that he has always made up his own mind, fought his own battles and stood his own ground without the props of Church, family or party politics to fall back upon in times of terror. ... [The captives'] tolerance of each other was the greatest act of inner defiance Keenan and McCarthy could have made in opposition to the fanatics who held them hostage.¹⁷

McGuinness here, of course, as in his play, leaves unexamined the entire notion of 'fanatic,' content merely to use the word to characterize the Other who are in 'opposition' to our friends the captives.

Not much happens in *Someone Who'll Watch Over Me*, which has neither plot nor really even story. In some ways, this is a Godot-like play in which nothing happens – twice – and audience members are likely to recall the wisdom of Dr. Johnston's advice to Thomas Erskine: 'Why, sir, if you were to read Richardson for the story your impatience would be so much fretted that you would hang yourself. But you must read him for the sentiment.' What we need to watch for in this nearly plotless play is not so much sentiment as ideas, and those ideas are revealed in part through patterns and contrasts of stereotypes. This somewhat artificial assemblage of three nationalities in the confines of a single room where they are chained to the wall and thus deprived of most movement allows McGuinness to bring the stereotypical characters into relation and to reveal both their conflicts with each other and the basic humanity that unites them.

This juxtaposition of stereotypes is paralleled and matched not just by the implicit Beirut/Belfast parallels, but also by McGuinness's use of a wide range of quotations and literary references. David Lloyd has pointed out how unsettling popular culture's 'processes of hybridization' are to both colonialists and nationalists. Popular culture's 'indifference to cultural hierarchies' allows it to mingle serious and burlesque, high and low, classical and contemporary, which tends to 'disintegrate' the cultural uniformity so important to both colonialists and nationalists.[18] McGuinness's inclusive style works in similar ways to disintegrate artificial cultural, social, and national boundaries.

Adam, for example, reads a passage from the Koran in which the emphasis on Peace is agonizingly familiar to a Christian ear. He reads passages from the Song of Solomon in which sacred and divine love are as closely mingled as they are in the George Herbert poem that Michael quotes later. (The program for the original production at the Hampstead Theatre quotes the lines that the text omits from this passage of the Song of Solomon – lines that compare the smell of the beloved's garments to the smell of Lebanon.) 'Sir Orfeo,' the Middle English poem based on the Orpheus legend, the biblical story of Ruth, and the hymn, 'Amazing Grace' (which has its own historic association with captivity) turn out to tell the same tale. And a passage from the Koran, in reminding us that 'over you there are watchers' (27), illuminates both Edward's watching over Adam at night and McGuinness's modification of the title of the Gershwin/Ella Fitzgerald song with which the play opens –

'Someone To Watch Over Me' – into the title of this play – *Someone Who'll Watch Over Me*.

At the end of Scene Five – which in production closed the first act – Adam sings a fuller version of 'Amazing Grace', the hymn he has been humming throughout. It is a powerful, resonant dramatic moment. Significantly, Adam does not sing the line 'I once was bound but now am free', but the hymn both encapsulates many of the themes that have come before and emphasizes the play's religious dimension. For this is, as both lead actor Stephen Rea[19] and critic Edith Oliver have pointed out, a 'religious play'.[20] It is religious in the broadest, least sectarian sense of the word. It is religious above all in the root sense of the word – to bind fast.[21]

Edward, like McGuinness himself, is a teacher of Old and Middle English, and that fact suggests another possible influence on the structure of this play. Medieval satires, of which Brant's fifteenth-century German allegory *Das Narrenschiff (The Ship of Fools)* is perhaps – thanks in part to Katherine Anne Porter – the best known, de-emphasized plot and relied heavily on caricature as they critiqued their society. The Ship of Fools carries an assortment of diverse individuals – united primarily by their foolishness – in a voyage to a 'fool's paradise'. It is the ship of the world on its way to eternity. McGuinness's characters are trapped not in the closed world of a ship, but in the closed world of a room which is really a cell. Recognizing their situation is a key element in their survival, and it is a telling moment in Michael's understanding when he moves from insistence that 'I have never been inside a prison and I never will be' (25) to acknowledgement that this room *is* a 'cell' (39).

The contrast between the notion of the world as a moving ship and the notion of world as an immobile cell is perhaps one indication of the difference between the medieval mind and the modern mind, but these prisoners are as clearly emblematic of the fate of the world as are the voyagers on the Ship of Fools. John Simon's suggestion that the invisible fourth wall of the theatre becomes the wall to which viewers are chained, 'imprisoned in [their own] existence',[22] is surely correct not just in its assessment of the power of this play but also in its implication that the prison shared by these ethnic stereotypes is a metaphor for the prison we all share in our wait for eternity.

Brant's depiction in *The Ship of Fools* of characters who are foolish both in their personal weaknesses and in their inability to understand the divine will fits McGuinness's play as well. Their captivity makes no sense to Adam, Edward, and Michael – or, for that matter, to most of us, I suspect. They can only repeat the word Edward has brought from Derry – 'Ridiculous, Ridiculous' (46). The word suggests both the bizarre humour of their situation and the limits of human wisdom. Presumably some day we will stand face to face. 'Ridiculous' is also close to 'absurd,' of course, and useful parallels can be drawn between this play and such earlier dramas as Samuel Beckett's *Endgame* (1956) and Sam Shepard's *Action* (1975)[23] – plays in which some sort of catastrophe has similarly cut characters off from the outside world and isolated them in a cramped interior. McGuinness's captives are trapped, partially immobilized (like Nagg and Nell), afraid of being left alone (like Hamm), and at the mercy of forces with unfathomable motives and unlimited power over them. Trapped in their post-apocalyptic world, they must face not only each other but also themselves. One way they do this is through creation of imaginary screenplays that – like the narratives created by characters in *Endgame* and *Action* – emphasize their own potential as actors in a fictional narrative.

In *Someone Who'll Watch Over Me*, the unseen captors are forces of power and control with rough but interesting parallels both with Beckett's Godot and with the Fates in Greek tragedy. Their existence and their power limit the extent to which tolerance becomes a hopeful response or 'solution' to life's troubles. Within the prison room, it is tolerance that sets the atmosphere in which support and love grow from and among differences, enabling these men to survive. Beyond this room, however, the world is Other: unknown, stereotyped and stereotyping, outside the realm of tolerance. Like Huck and Jim floating down the Mississippi on the raft, creating a mutually-supportive world in opposition to the destructive forces on shore, these captives are isolated in a special but limited realm of tolerance and good will.

References to fate run like a leitmotif through this play, setting the existential situation to which the prisoners, like all humans, must respond. 'Whoever has no control', says Adam, 'is fucked. I am American, I am Arab. I am fucked. We have that much in common' (22). But if God is not, as the Koran promises, 'the merciful, the compassionate', Edward tells Adam, then they must 'Face up to [our] fate' (28). To Adam's suggestion that they are at the Arabs' mercy, Edward responds, 'We're at our own' (28), thus insisting on their ultimate responsibility as actors in a profoundly inexplicable world. In so far as the play posits a solution, then, it is a solution to an existential dilemma, not a solution to social or political problems. Tolerance does not touch the ridiculous world that traps these men. Tolerance does enable them to deal with that unchanging external situation by tapping what is best in human nature.

Michael professes a preference for the 'essential optimism of the medieval mind and its profound faith in human happiness to triumph over despair,' suggesting he finds the optimistic medieval mind 'much deeper than Renaissance doubt' (37). Though the play, like Michael, may occasionally reveal a lack of faith, its final scene juxtaposes many of the work's most powerfully positive images. Edward, who is being released, is saying good-bye to Michael, and he assures him that Adam is 'watching over us' (57) and that 'I'm watching over you' (58). He also, imitating a gesture Michael has told him was typical of Spartans going into battle, leans over and combs Michael's hair. Then Michael combs his. It is an action of remarkable tenderness and love, epitomizing the power of touch that has been largely denied to these prisoners chained to the wall – and it comes from the character who seemed initially just another incarnation of the stage Irishman. Michael, left alone, repeats lines from the Old English poem 'The Wanderer', which he has quoted before.

> Oft him anhaga are gebideth. Wyrd bith ful araed. (58)

A man who is alone may at times feel mercy, mercy towards himself.... Fate is fate (51).

He also quotes the Biblical Ruth, who, as Julia Kristeva points out, epitomizes the 'unity' that 'can be achieved only if an exterior, an 'outside of,' is joined to the 'same'. [24]

> Whither thou goest, I will go with thee, and whither I go, thou shalt go with me. (58)

Like Adam's singing of 'Amazing Grace' at the close of the first act, this moment is a dramatically powerful encapsulation of the play's religious dimension and unusual optimism. The fates of these captives may not seem particularly triumphant – one dead, one released, one still in captivity. In the larger world of understanding and love, however, they have indeed triumphed. They have defeated despair with love and compassion. They have laughed at, with, and through caricature and stereotype to discover what is most deeply similar and human about themselves.

Typically an ethnic joke places members of different cultures in an identical situation so that their differences may be illuminated by their varying responses to a fixed situation.[25] This play moves in precisely the opposite direction. The ethnic stereotypes move through the differences that divide to discover the similarity that unites – a shared capacity for caring and love. That capacity will not solve the world's problems, but it comes close to the medieval 'profound faith in human happiness to triumph over despair' (37). That faith is perhaps a faith with which humans can live, or die, or even remain in the limbo of captivity. As McGuinness said of Keenan's book, 'From this horror has come something wonderful.'[26]

---

[1] Frank McGuinness, *Someone Who'll Watch Over Me* (London: Faber and Faber, 1992). Subsequent references are to this edition; page citations are given in parentheses.

[2] Harry Haun, 'A Rea of Starlight,' Playbill: The Booth Theatre, February 1993, p.8. This description itself seems unconsciously to reflect common American assumptions about other nationalities. Both the Irishman and the Englishman get stereotypical adjec-

tives, and the Englishman gets the often pejorative diminutive 'Brit' as well. Only the American's description is neutral.

3 For fuller analysis of ethnic jokes and language, see Alan Dundes, *Cracking Jokes: Studies of Sick Humour Cycles and Stereotypes* (Berkeley, 1987; Irving Lewis Allen, *The Language of Ethnic Conflict* (New York, 1983); and Rosemary Gordon, *Stereotype of Imagery and Belief as an Ego Defense* (Cambridge, 1962).

4 The text does not specify Adam's ethnicity. The idea of casting an African American in the role seems not to have originated with McGuinness. The Irish premiere did not cast an African American in the role.

5 Seamus Deane, 'Introduction', *Nationalism, Colonialism, and Literature* (Minneapolis: Field Day, 1990), pp.12-13.

6 See Wolfgang Stroebe and Chester A. Insko, 'Stereotype, Prejudice, and Discrimination: Changing Conceptions in Theory and Research' in *Stereotyping and Prejudice: Changing Conceptions*, ed. Daniel Bar-Tal and others (New York, 1889).

7 See Susan T. Fiske and Steven L. Neuberg, 'Category-Based and Individuating Processes as a Function of Information and Motivation: Evidence from Our Laboratory' for a fuller discussion of the connections between stereotypes and dependence. They conclude that perceivers are more likely to avoid stereotyping when they are 'motivated to be accurate, perhaps by being outcome dependent on the target.' In *Stereotyping and Prejudice*, p.100.

8 For fuller discussion of the development of 'social cohesion and social order' by transmitting general values 'through socialization processes', see Stroebe and Insko. Allen considers in detail the use of stereotypes to 'exert social control' and 'demarcate boundaries' between groups. See pp.14-15 esp.

9 Edward W. Said, *Covering Islam: How the Media and the Experts Determine How We See the Rest of the World* (New York, 1981), p.39. See also Said's Culture and Imperialism (London, 1993).

10 Julia Kristeva, *Strangers to Ourselves*, trans. Leon S. Roudiez (New York, 1991), p.1.

11 'Keenan Tells of a Hostage's 'Crucifying Aloneness," *Irish Times*, 31 August 1990, p.4.

12 Brian Keenan, *An Evil Cradling* (London, 1992), p.xii. Subsequent references are to this edition; page citations are given in parentheses.

13 Seamus Heaney, 'Whatever You Say Say Nothing', in *North* (London, 1975), pp.57-60.
14 'The Sense of Place' in *Preoccupations: Selected Prose, 1968-1978* (London, 1980), p.131.
15 Deane, p.18.
16 *Culture and Imperialism* (London, 1993), p.285.
17 Frank McGuinness, 'The Unforgotten Men in the Oubliette' *Irish Times*, 26 September 1992, p.9.
18 David Lloyd, *Anomalous States: Irish Writing and the Post-Colonial Moment* (Dublin, 1993), pp.95 and 96.
19 Haun, p.8
20 Edith Oliver, 'Cellmates', *New Yorker*, 7 December 1992, p.154.
21 See *The Oxford Dictionary of English Etymology*. The *OED* cites a more complex etymology, but indicates that modern writers favour the 'bind fast' sense because it explains the force of the word.
22 John Simon, 'Stout Fellow, McGuinness!' *New York*, 7 December 1992, p.68.
23 Actor Stephen Rea, who played Edward in the London and New York productions of *Someone Who'll Watch Over Me*, played Shooter in the original 1974 production of *Action*.
24 Kristeva, p.69.
25 Dundes, p.120.
26 'The Unforgotten Man in the Oubliette'.

Self-Dramatization in the Plays of Frank McGuinness*

Joan FitzPatrick Dean

Few modern dramatists have created characters as varied or have drawn upon situations as diverse as Frank McGuinness. Over the past two decades McGuinness has written about expressly Irish situations – the 'Troubles' in Northern Ireland in *Carthaginians* (1988) and the zealous patriotism of Northern Irishmen who fought in World War I in *Observe the Sons of Ulster Marching Towards the Somme* (1985) – as well as more international, if not universal, predicaments like homelessness in *Baglady* (1982) and terrorism in *Someone Who'll Watch Over Me* (1992). His plays portray the lives of ordinary as well as extraordinary people. Set in McGuinness's native county and country or in Italy, Beirut, and France, his characters find themselves in the sixteenth century, the second decade of this century, or, more frequently, in our own day. Some of the plays are based on momentous historical situations; others draw upon his own experience; still others, like *Peer Gynt* (1988), are adaptations often having a distinct analogue to a contemporary situation – especially to one in Ireland.

As they struggle with questions of identity, questions central to modern Irish literature, McGuinness's characters define and

---

* *This article first appeared in* New Hibernia Review *3:1 (Spring 1999), pp.97-110.*

re-create themselves and move beyond the simplicities of dichotomous choices to the far more ambiguous complexities of sexual, gender, and familial identity. Of the Englishman and the Irishman in *Someone Who'll Watch Over Me*, Helen Lojek observes: 'McGuinness has created characters who have taken possession of their stereotypes and are no longer bound by them.'[1] To overstate the importance of nationality or religion is dangerously misleading because McGuinness's plays are no less concerned with other sources and forms of identity: sexual orientation, gender, class, and age. McGuinness's emphasis typically falls on the paradoxes of identity and freedom, essence and existence.

The question of identity occupies a pre-eminent place in Irish writing and its criticism. Gerald Dawe begins *Against Piety* (1995), his recent book on modern Irish poetry, with the issue of identity, with specific reference to Thomas Kinsella's views: 'The freedom, the *necessary* freedom, Kinsella suggests, is for the writer to choose an imaginative identity and, if that identity is framed by an inappropriate tradition, then it is the writer's responsibility to create an alternative tradition that is liberating.'[2] Wrenched from their traditions, McGuinness's characters assert their identity through self-dramatization – the characters' creation and performance of versions of themselves. His characters routinely draw upon and define themselves through extradramatic or metadramatic devices. These include game playing, nomination (the act of renaming people and things), the re-enactment of historical and personal events, role playing, and plays-within-plays – as well as such intertextual devices as storytelling, recitation, song, and the retelling of dreams. All of these dramatic tactics share two non-naturalistic qualities. First, they necessarily involve an element of artifice in that they are 'scripted,' non-spontaneous or performances, theatrical by their very nature. Second, because they elicit a tension between the self and a persona, all play on that disparity – between the 'true' character and the storyteller or between the self and the game player. McGuinness sees this use of theatricality as part of his heritage: 'One of the major assets you have as an Irish writer is that when an Irish audience comes to the theatre they are expecting to see in a play from Synge onwards – well, from Farquhar – a sense of the innate theatricality of life, so that an Irish audience will accept very willingly a play-within-a-play.'[3] McGuinness's use of masks, intertextuality, and persona all tap this innate theatricality to draw on what Johan Huizinga's description in *Homo Ludens* of man as a game-player: 'The player, withdrawn from the ordinary world by the mask he wore, felt himself transformed into another ego which he did not so much represent as incarnate and actualize.'[4]

Dramatists from Shakespeare to Stoppard have employed techniques of self-dramatization often, but not invariably, to comic ends. Although typically humorous, these jokes, stories, playlets, and games of self-dramatization are neither simple comic relief nor digressions; rather, they are the strategies of self-discovery and survival. Not only is self-dramatization McGuinness's central strategy of characterization, it also shapes his thematic treatment of identity and underscores his emphasis on the transformative powers of laughter and imagination.

Like self-dramatization, situations of isolation and duress are typical in McGuinness's plays. Riana O'Dwyer notes that McGuinness's characters exist 'outside the domestic sphere' in a public area she identifies as a 'borderland'.[5] Death, grief, and guilt have cut off the links to previous identities for the characters in a Derry cemetery in *Carthaginians*. First boot camp and, later, the horrors of trench warfare isolate the characters in *Observe the Sons of Ulster*. No less extreme is the situation of the American, Irishman, and Englishman chained to the wall by terrorists in *Someone Who'll Watch Over Me*. Under duress, the simplicities of identity are tested and found wanting; characters are forced to re-create and often redefine themselves. Isolation not only cuts the characters off from their previous lives, it also brings together individuals who otherwise would have little contact. In a Derry cemetery, Roman Catholics share their grief with Protestants, and a fifty-year-old mother can be cared for by a drag queen. Unquestioning Unionists enlist in the same army as self-destructive cynics. Family and home hold great importance, but more for their absence than their presence. Under such isolation and duress, the dichotomies that hold sway over so much modern Irish expression and its criticism break down. Especially in game playing, self-dramatization compounds the possibilities of identity well beyond binary opposites. Questions of sexuality or gender preference offer even greater ambiguity of identity. That McGuinness is both Irish and gay makes this process of self-dramatization especially resonant.

Typically, McGuinness's characters find themselves in largely static situations. In many of his plays, as in many of Beckett's, nothing happens.[6] His, like Beckett's, are characters *in extremis.* Poverty, war, grief, or imprisonment deny them the supports for identity traditionally found in family, community, or nation. Characters may be immobilized physically by imprisonment, grief, or authority, but their physical constraint only intensifies the relentless mobility of their thoughts. By situating his characters in circumstances as static as they are desperate, McGuinness rejects the formulaic strategies of suspense and action of the familiar well-made play. Not surprisingly, the dramaturgy appropriate to illustrate the paradoxes of freedom and identity is rarely naturalistic and is predicated even more rarely upon conventional conflict and action. Instead of dramatizing the inevitability of his characters' identities, McGuinness dramatizes their choice of identity. Although largely straightforward in their dramaturgy and linear chronology, McGuinness's first plays deal explicitly with characters who attempt to fashion an identity in an unfamiliar setting. Even in his earliest play McGuinness thrusts characters into situations in which they must reinvent themselves. The women in *The Factory Girls*, a naturalistic treatment of social problems, leave their domestic situations first for tedious labour outside the home. Then, assuming powers they might never have imagined having, they occupy the office of their boss. In later plays, the past, the sense of home, traditions and familiar pieties are irreparably disrupted – even the most intimate relationships of his characters.

In *Innocence*, Caravaggio invites and welcomes that disruption as he attempts to create himself, not least by denying his past and his family. He lives in Rome, far removed from his family and his roots. His names reveal the effort to create a new identity. Although Lena and others refer to him as 'Lello', Caravaggio repeatedly defines himself by reciting his litany of names: 'Michelangelo for the angel ... Merisi for my family and Caravaggio for the birthplace of my father.'[7] He tells the Cardinal that his family is dead, but as McGuinness has said of Caravaggio,

> He's creating a new self for himself and art of that creation is the denial of family. And as we know [for] anybody foolish enough to do that, the family will catch up with you.[8]

When his brother appears with news of their sister's death in childbirth, Caravaggio's newly minted identity begins to unravel.

That his beloved sister died in giving birth underscores the inclusive vision of *Innocence*: death entails birth; darkness light. Caravaggio tells the Cardinal, whom he serves as both pimp and painter, that 'All life is death, all light is darkness, and from the darkness your boys have crawled to bring you the light of love' (*I* 24). Although Caravaggio is homosexual, that hardly precludes his wish to see his family's line continued. He urges his brother to leave the priesthood and to have children. He and Lena fantasize about having children: 'Two, hundred, thousand, a million' (*I* 6). Much later, Lena urges him not to accept an identity that is based on a lie: 'See the queer. See his darkness. See yourself' (*I* 48). In Caravaggio's dream, the ghost of his sister Caterina commands him to 'live' (*I* 58), affirming the value of life no matter what the circumstances. At the play's end, having killed Rannuccio Tomassoni, Caravaggio sets out to reinvent himself anew. Lena's parting words to Caravaggio encapsulate the antithetical voices of romantic love and street slang:

> When death comes no matter where we are, be one alive or not, be one there or not, we will die in each other's arms, and I will shed sore tears to leave you alone. Now fuck off.(*I* 59)

The dream sequence in *Innocence* in which Caravaggio's sister appears is an important departure from naturalistic dramaturgy. In subsequent plays, McGuinness regularly employs a fluid, episodic form that accommodates the movement through time and space while, with the exception of *Mary and Lizzie*, maintaining a strong foothold in realism, especially psychological realism. Unlike many of Beckett's stage characters, McGuinness's inhabit a very specific time and place; they are, moreover, highly individualized and psychologically complex. For example, in *Baglady*, McGuinness reveals character not through conventional conflict, but through self-dramatization - here through the expressionistic monologue of an eponymous character. Like Tom o' Bedlam in Shakespeare's *King Lear*, the Baglady is mad, homeless, and utterly 'unaccommodated' by society and its institutions. Her presence on stage reveals a lifetime of abuse that stripped her of home, family, and identity, and reduced her to penury. Dislocated from all that was once familiar, her identity, like her child, has been drowned. In her conflation of past and present, time has lost its potential to order her experience. As memories from her youth flood back on her, she uses the present tense to describe her father as 'a respected man, a decent man ... a good man ... a gentleman.'[9] but the audience learns that her father raped her and is long since dead. Like Shakespeare's Poor Tom, she is fixated on the horrific experiences she cannot escape.

The Baglady's storytelling, which initially seems to be no less grotesque than her physical appearance, pivots around the death of her child. She can tell her story only indirectly – by letting the cards, which she associates with her mother, speak for her. Through her fragmentary memories, the outline of a traumatic narrative of incest emerges: her father raped her; the priest disbelieved her story; her son was taken from her and drowned. She was cautioned not to tell, but acts of telling dominate the play. Insisting 'I'm going to tell, I'm going to tell' (B 77), she makes the very act of telling her rebellion, her self-assertion, her identity. And like Poor Tom, ordinary language cannot adequately express her terror. McGuinness says of her that 'Baglady is attempting to find a language for the wrong that has been done to her. And if she can find that language, she'll be at peace.'[10] Her self-dramatization remains oblique, grounded in a story that only the cards rather than her own voice can relate. Like the Baglady, the Elder Pyper in *Observe the*

Sons of Ulster is extremely reluctant to revisit the formative experiences that now imprison him.

Kenneth Pyper appears in two incarnations – old and young. That the roles are played by two different actors underscores how profoundly unlike the young man the Elder Pyper is. The two appearances of Old Pyper look back to and frame the three scenes, 'Initiation,' 'Pairing,' and 'Bonding,' set in 1916. As a young man, Pyper plays at various roles and poses, offering all sorts of possibilities, but after the death of his friends at the Battle of the Somme, he knows exactly who he is. Defined by the bigotry that perversely honours the memories of his comrades, the identity of the Elder Pyper is absolutely rigid, set in stone – the very medium in which the Younger Pyper worked as a sculptor.

The indeterminacy of the Younger Pyper's identity is evident in his manipulation of names. He first pretends to be a superior officer; moments later he introduces himself as 'David Craig,' and much later, when Craig and Pyper are on Boa Island, Craig reaffirms the bond of identification between them by telling Pyper 'I am you.'[11] The Younger Pyper plays yet another role when he introduces himself as a stage magician; 'Let me entertain you' (*OSU* 34) he says, moments before punching Anderson in the groin and putting a stop to his game of sniffing out Catholics.

Not only does the Younger Pyper juggle names and identities, but an extensive repertoire of intricately tabulated stories as well. In one he says he married 'a Papist whore ... out of curiosity ... to make an honest Protestant out of her' (*OSU* 29). Spinning a tale as Christy Mahon might, the Younger Pyper tells his audience of fellow enlistees that she fulfilled even their most grotesque fantasies about the anatomical peculiarities of Catholics by revealing 'three legs. The middle one shorter than the normal two' (*OSU* 30). He also tells of a time in France when he nearly starved and made a covenant never to return to Ireland, but then grew wings and flew home. The Younger Pyper's gnomic, contradictory explorations through self-dramatization attest to the power of imagination to create a reality that is as powerful as it is revelatory. In the Elder Pyper, who appears at the beginning in 'Remembrance' and not again until the last twenty lines of the play, these polymorphous possibilities have disappeared completely.

From what the Elder Pyper says at the very beginning of *Observe the Sons of Ulster*, he is stuck in the past. Confined to a wheelchair as surely as he is immobilized in the past, he tries to deny his memory and laments the cycle in which he has entrapped himself. 'Again. As always, again. Why does this persist?' (*OSU* 9). Reluctant to speak of his experience, the Elder Pyper cannot awake from a militant Unionist's version of what Joyce's Stephen Dedalus calls 'the nightmare of history.'[12] Unlike his young self, the Elder Pyper has in fact so delimited his nature, his beliefs, his personality, that he has attained absolute certitude and, with that certitude, total stasis. McGuinness has said he knew Pyper's last line 'would be 'I love my Ulster' and I knew that I had to get a character that would find that as hard to say as I would find it.'[13] McGuinness's considerable task, then, is to reveal how a character of his own creation might come to hold monstrous and barbaric beliefs, ones that abominate the likes of Frank McGuinness, as articles of faith. In fact, *Observe the Sons of Ulster* renders the Elder Pyper's bigotry neither tolerable nor acceptable, but intelligible. So burdensome is the nightmare of history for the Elder Pyper that he has arrived at a state of life-in-death, saying he 'died' that day with his comrade and friend David Craig. The Elder Pyper gives meaning to his friends' deaths in assuming a fixed identity that admits no possibility of change, only the stasis of identity that is here, as elsewhere in McGuinness, synonymous with death. Having failed in his relationship with the French woman, having failed in his art, having failed to die in battle, the Elder Pyper abandons his poses and indeterminacy and takes up his death-in-life sentence. Once the master of revels, but now immobilized in a wheelchair, he can admit no ambiguity, no laughter, no imagination. His last line is not, in fact, 'I love my Ulster', but 'Dance', and it returns us to Carson's triumphalist dance of Protestant bigotry.

Hardly confined to Pyper, self-dramatization appears among virtually all the characters in *Observe the Sons of Ulster*. Hymns and songs regularly punctuate the dialogue. As the eight young men from different parts of Ulster assemble in boot camp, they reveal a striking diversity of temperament and background.[14] All, save Pyper, serve to prove their loyalty to king and country, but Anderson and McIlwaine also serve to gratify their self-definition as triumphalist Protestants, and, therefore, haters of Catholics. Two Belfast bullies, Anderson and McIlwaine, stage their game of 'I spy a Taig' (*OSU* 33), the latter taking the part of a mad attack dog. Later, they try to re-enact the July 12 Orange march they missed while away from Ireland. Crawford and Rowlston, like the Younger Pyper, enlist to escape the past. Like McGuinness's Caravaggio, all three obscure and deny their pasts in the hope of reinventing themselves. Other characters reveal their hopes and fears in recounting their dreams and, in 'Pairing,' all eight play out their fears and fantasies.

In 'Bonding', the play's final scene, McGuinness uses burlesque retellings and re-enactments of events to establish the characters' perceptions of their historical context. For McIlwaine, the Easter Rising is a laughable episode, proof that 'Fenians can't fight ... [and are a] disgrace to their sex' (*OSU* 64-5). His retelling reduces events in Dublin to a joke in which 'this boy Pearse' runs out of stamps and was then shot by his mother for holding up a post office. More ominous for these eight men is their historical re-enactment, in distinctively burlesque fashion, of the confrontation between William of Orange and King James at the Battle of the Boyne. With Roulston on Pyper's shoulders, as King Billy astride his white horse, and Moore, as King James, on Millen's shoulders, the mock re-enactment comes to a prophetic end when Pyper stumbles – King James is seen to win the battle. Their triumphalism will end in their death at the Battle of the Somme, but endure in the Elder Pyper.

Like *Observe the Sons of Ulster*, *Carthaginians* focuses not on the political and military events that occupy most historians, as well as a few poets and playwrights – the Battle of the Somme, Bloody Sunday, the Easter Rising. *Carthaginians* looks instead at the consequences, the personal heritage of those events for those who remain alive. And, like *Innocence* and *Mary and Lizzie*,

Carthaginians demonstrates that death may be a more alluring and even an easier choice than life. In *Carthaginians*, which McGuinness hopes audiences see as a companion piece to *Observe the Sons of Ulster*,[15] the characters pass a week, beginning on Monday morning, waiting in a Derry cemetery for the raising of the dead. Paul is building a pyramid 'through [which] the dead will find their way back to the world.'[16] Theirs is a figurative imprisonment in grief, regret, or guilt. Outcasts where they should be most at home, these characters, like the Baglady, exist on the very margins of a city – in this case, Derry – itself a war zone.

Although Hark, Paul, and Seph knew each other before Bloody Sunday, *Carthaginians* brings together an unlikely assembly of other characters who have no place left to them. The audience is denied any systematic exposition, yet it learns that what brings and binds these characters together is summed up in Hark's belief that Bloody Sunday left 'Only the dead and the dying' (*C* 66). For Seph, who is reduced to silence in the play's first scenes – and speaks only to stop Hark from beating Dido (*C* 66) – life itself is his punishment

> I talked. I ran away. And I came back. I went to those I informed on. I said 'Kill me. Let me die.' They said, 'Live. That's your sentence. Life, not death. Live with what you've done.' (*C* 44-45)

Paul, to whom Derry has 'grown foreign,' is driven mad by the 'war in my head' (*C* 60). John Harkin once was 'Johnny,' but since has informed, or at least given information on his friends under questioning, 'Johnny is dead now and only Harkin remains. That's all that's left. The rest is dead.' Hark served a term in prison for what Paul describes as a less than heroic involvement in his cause: 'You never volunteered .... A glorified look-out man who got himself caught' (*C* 62). A reformed heroin addict, Sarah has come back to Derry to be with Hark. Greta, who lives in the house in which she grew up, is described by Seph as hating herself. In her songs about her imaginary 'dead' brother, she agonizes over her inability to come to terms with her sexual identity. Greta is perhaps as much at home in the cemetery as she might be anywhere in Derry. More is revealed about Maela, whose daughter died of cancer on Bloody Sunday. Refusing to accept that her daughter's body is in her coffin, Maela continues to knit a sweater for her twenty-ninth birthday. All that is known about Dido is Maela saved him from suicide; they then teamed up as Oldie and Goldie for, of all things, table quizzes. Removed from Derry's domestic and social structures – ones they might accept or rebel against – that would provide them with a sense of identity, this entirely unlikely group of misfits bands together in an ersatz family. Having failed to re-invent themselves within the confines of society, they are all outcasts from the pieties and conventions of the mainstream – exactly the sort of characters toward whom McGuinness gravitates.[17]

As they keep their vigil for the resurrection of the dead, they pass the time like Beckett's Vladimir and Estragon. They indulge in parody, game-playing, and self-determination. McGuinness's characters chant football cheers and sing 'We Shall Overcome,' 'In the Port of Amsterdam', and, perhaps most memorably, the theme song from 'The Flintstones'. Here intertextuality affirms the characters' freedom and injects comedy into a profoundly grim situation. Like the characters in *Observe the Sons of Ulster*, as well as those in *Someone Who'll Watch Over Me*, they offer clues to their identities by relating their dreams. Greta imagines herself the brother she did not have; Sarah's dream takes her back to her drug addiction in imagining that her veins were full of money (*C* 30). Dido's dream starts out as a licentious fantasy about a gorgeous Lebanese sailor, but ends with the belief that the earth will no longer accept those who have died in the violence (*C* 28–29). Likewise, one of the most revealing links among these disparate and desperate characters is that they are inveterate gamesters, particularly drawn to table quizzes, whose structure is the basis of much of the play's dialogue.

> **Paul:** What city did Rome destroy?
> **Greta:** Carthage.
> **Paul:** Correct. Two points. Carthage.
> **Greta:** How are we in Carthage?

Paul: Tell them you saw sitting in the ruins, in the graveyard. (*C* 17)[18]

The central episode of self-dramatization in *Carthaginians* is the acting of Dido's postmodern polemic 'The Burning Balaclava'. Recognizing the cathartic potential for drama, Dido offers the mourners a sensational melodrama written under the pseudonym Fionnula McGonigle, whose initials, not coincidentally, are those of Dido's creator. A formal play-within-the-play, 'The Burning Balaclava' evokes the comparison with the production of 'Pyramus and Thisby' in Shakespeare's *A Midsummer Night's Dream*. Both stand as an ironic comment on the play, not least by turning tragedy into comedy. As in *A Midsummer Night's Dream*, non-actors are enlisted for this read-through. In Shakespeare, of course, men do play women's roles, much to the consternation of young Flute: 'faith let me not play a woman. I have a beard coming.'[19] In the Derry cemetery, men play women, women play men, and Dido, like Bottom, offers to play more than one part.[20]

Dido's play is populated by Derry residents all of whom have slight variations on the same surname: Doherty, O'Dochartaigh, Dogherty, O'Doherty. Its plot is no less improbable. In fanatic devotion to the Sacred Heart, the fifty-year-old mother Doherty, now neglects her son, 'patriot and idealist' Padraig O'Dochartaigh, whose girlfriend, Doreen Dogherty, is the daughter of a Royal Ulster Constabulary officer. While walking her dog, Doreen meets a British soldier who shoots and then starts kicking Doreen's dog. The roles of Doreen and soldier are both played by Dido, alternatively wearing a beret and an army helmet. Although Doreen and Padraig hope for a better world in the future, 'a [new] province where Catholics and Protestants can go to bed together and talk dirty' (*C* 39), their situation quickly devolves into a confrontation with Doreen and her RUC father on one side, Padraig and his mother on other. To the accompaniment of 'Do Not Forsake Me' from *High Noon*, the two families face each other in a shootout with water pistols.

When Dido asks 'Isn't it just like real life?' Hark, Sarah, Paul, Greta, and Maela unanimously denounce the play as 'Shite ... Shite incredible. Shite incarnate' (*C* 43). These characters will not support the comfortable illusions that ordinarily create easy identities, nor will they endure the ludicrous caricatures of Dido's opus. Through the play-within-the-play, McGuinness examines the relationship between art and life. Like the rehearsal of 'Pyramus and Thisby' by Shakespeare's rude mechanicals, this reading of 'The Burning Balaclava' exposes the assumptions and limits of drama as a mimetic art. Art may uplift, console or explicate a problem. It may even be beautiful, but it cannot provide a definite answer, nor will it solve a problem. The play-within-the-play suggests the misplaced focus of drama that dwells on a realistic representation of a historical event.

Even so, after Dido's exit, the characters reassess his play; it is good *craic*. 'Even old Seph enjoyed himself.' (*C* 44) Impossibly, the play-within-the-play realizes drama's potential to unite its audience and to achieve the catharsis of life-affirming laughter. And that is precisely what Dido intended. As Christopher Murray remarks, 'More Dionysus than drag queen, Dido creates the possibility for renewal through art.'[21] That possibility for renewal is what McGuinness creates as well. The final recitation in *Carthaginians*, though, is the mournful litany of the names, addresses, and ages of those who died on Bloody Sunday. At the very end of the play, Dido, having chosen to move away from Derry, takes his leave of the others by commanding them to 'Play'. (*C* 70) In contrast to the immobilized Pyper, Dido is the model of freedom, energy, mobility, and creativity. *Carthaginians*, unlike *Observe the Sons of Ulster*, poses the choice between life and death.

The redemptive comic spirit of *Carthaginians* also pervades *Someone Who'll Watch Over Me* and works against all that we might expect from a play about three hostages held by terrorists in Beirut. McGuinness's play is filled with jokes – one-liners, riddles, shaggy-dog stories. *Someone Who'll Watch Over Me* also contains more songs than *Carthaginians*: 'Amazing Grace,' 'Chitty Chitty, Bang Bang,' 'The Water is Wide,' 'Run Rabbit

Run Rabbit,' and of course 'Someone To Watch Over Me' – as well as recitations from the Bible, the Koran, and 'The Wanderer.'

The play's three hostages are initially described in terms of their nationality – Irish, American, and English – so even the basic situation recalls a joke. But those labels are hardly definitive and are, in fact, quickly eclipsed both by the characters' individuality and by their common experience of imprisonment. The choice between mutually exclusive categories or labels owing everything to the circumstances of birth and parentage – American, Irish or English; rural or urban; rich or poor; even black or white[22] – is less than central to the characters in *Carthaginians* and *Someone Who'll Watch Over Me*. Even in desperate circumstances, McGuinness's characters discover significant freedoms and, with those freedoms, responsibilities, especially in regard to identity.[23]

In *Someone Who'll Watch Over Me*, Edward's Northern Irish accent, his idiomatic use of language, his profound and caustic sense of irony, his faith in laughter, and his sometimes obvious anger all mark him as Irish and distinguish him from the decorous Englishman and the self-made American. Edward refers more often to his native land than do Michael or Adam, and from him we hear about Strabane, Omagh, Belfast, and Derry. Moreover, he is the one who most plainly suggests that his life will change after his imprisonment: he now wants to know his children, wants another child. Adam, the American, is self-reliant, forward-looking, devoted to optimism and self-improvement. Michael is unapologetic and even proud of being English because of the nation's literature and, not least, because the tennis player Virginia Wade is English. He prides himself on civility, self-discipline, control. They are, in fact, all proud of their nationalities and openly defensive when ridiculed or challenged on that basis.

In *Someone Who'll Watch Over Me*, the characters offer one another instances of self-dramatization as momentary escapes from the tedium of imprisonment. They compose letters to their families. They sing, recite, recall, imagine. They create themselves and, in so doing, maintain their sanity and assert their freedom. Like Caravaggio, whose art is transformation, they appreciate how these excursions can transform their harsh reality. In the circumstances of their imprisonment, any assertion of identity or individuality – singing, laughing, even exercising – is a defiance of their captors. Like Dido, they recognize the importance of play in all its forms. For instance, 'Shoot the movie', a collaborative, progressive story, initiates the newly captured Michael to the regime of game playing that has sustained Edward and Adam. Adam narrates a Hitchcock version of Michael's arrival and capture in Beirut. Edward picks up the thread in a ridiculous pastiche of Sam Peckinpah and Richard Attenborough in which a nun, played by Madonna, comes to Beirut to work in orphanages, but is killed and later eaten by vultures.

How fully characters can recast reality and assert their own identity is evident in their self-dramatization. The episode of letter writing – an imaginary exercise, as they have neither pen nor paper – is directed more at one another than at their supposed addressees. Adam writes his fiancée and father. Edward's letter to his wife demonstrates his recognition of how little he has known or appreciated his family. Michael writes his 'Mum' that he is 'often flooded by a torrent of emotions, which I rise above.'[24] Though the drinks Edward serves up – vodka martini, large sherry, Guinness – are all no less imaginary than the pen and paper, they offer another escape. Although Michael, the Englishman, insists on the importance of control, he provides several of the most creative of the many performances embedded in the play. Michael stresses the importance of naming by insisting that he is in a 'room' not a 'cell' (*S* 25). The most expansive instance of self-dramatization is Michael's re-enactment of Virginia Wade's victory over Betty Stove in the 1977 Wimbeldon Ladies' Final. Edward, the Irishman, then takes the unlikely role of Queen Elizabeth in presenting Virginia with her award. Finally, on Christmas Day, Edward presents Michael with a special gift: an automobile that will carry them through London on an imaginary car ride from the film *Chitty Chitty, Bang Bang*.

Here, as in *Carthaginians*, where Maela rejoiced 'Thank God we can laugh'(*C* 9), the comic spirit that informs the play is essential to the characters' identities and survival. Edward sees laughter as the prisoners' refuge and defense: 'That's how we get by. Laughing at it all.' Adam corroborates this, saying 'Don't weep. That's what they want. So don't cry. Laugh.' (*S* 11) The three laugh for their guards not only as an alternative to weeping, but also as an assertion of their solidarity and humanity. The same action is repeated at the end of the play when Edward breaks down and Michael demands that he laugh.

These dramatic situations and modes of characterization again evoke Beckett's *Waiting for Godot*. Vladimir and Estragon define themselves through jokes, games, role playing, and other modes of self-dramatization. Both Beckett and McGuinness face the dramatic challenge to develop character in situations that fundamentally preclude the contrived conflict of the well-made play. In *Someone Who'll Watch Over Me*, although there is a level of tension between the visible prisoners and their unseen captors, virtually all of the conflicts on stage occur among the versions of themselves that McGuinness's prisoners create in the course of their own self-dramatization. Edward's departure entails a finality because it precludes the continuation of the performances that have given McGuinness's stage prisoners their camaraderie, hope, and laughter.

At the end of *The Myth of Sisyphus*, Albert Camus writes that, as Sisyphus walks down the mountain to resume his unending task, 'one must imagine Sisyphus happy,' for in those moments the gods who have sentenced him to this cruel labour can control neither his thoughts nor emotions.[25] That scintilla of freedom is enough for Camus to see freedom as intrinsic to the human condition. McGuinness's plays corroborate this conclusion. As Michael says of the terrorists who guard the hostages in *Someone Who'll Watch Over Me*, 'They have to do as they're told. I do as I choose.' The hostages in Beirut, like their counterparts in the Derry cemetery, create amusement, comedy, and, most importantly, they create themselves. The result of the characters' self-dramatization and rich theatricality, laughter is not only salutary but redemptive, and not least for McGuinness's audiences.

In McGuinness's recurrent situations of duress and isolation, death seems a more alluring choice than life. In *Mary and Lizzie*, the sisters descend into the underworld to visit their mother and are tempted to remain. In *Carthaginians*, Seph asks for death. The Elder Pyper says he 'died' with David Craig. Irrespective of the class, gender, age, or occupation, McGuinness's characters face what Camus saw as the only philosophical question – the choice of life or death. McGuinness's characters bring with them the baggage of the past, but they invariably live cut off from the comfortable familiarity of the past, from the identities with which they grew up. Through selfhood, song, memory, compassion, they escape confinement by suggesting possibilities in a dramaturgy that is, by definition, not realistic. Michael prides himself on his restraint, but he zestfully conjures up Virginia Wade to trounce 'poor wee Betty Stove' in the Wimbledon finals. Taken out of a social and personal context, individual identity is tested by the dislocation brought on by war, death, captivity, or guilt. That dislocation very often entails a literal or figurative imprisonment, but it can also carry the freedom to, as Dido urges, 'play' – to explore possibilities through self-dramatization, to pursue the realm of freedom that Camus imagined for Sisyphus.

[1] Helen Lojek, 'Watching Over Frank McGuinness's Stereotypes', *Modern Drama*, 38 (1995), p.350.
[2] Gerald Dawe, *Against Piety: Essays in Irish Poetry* (Belfast: Lagan Press, 1991), p.19.
[3] 'Frank McGuinness: A Profile', interview with Richard Pine, *Irish Literary Supplement* (Spring 1991), p.29.
[4] Johan Huizinga, *Homo Ludens: A Study of the Play Element in Culture* (Boston: Beacon Press, 1950), p.145.
[5] Riana O'Dwyer, 'Dancing in the Borderlands: The Plays of Frank McGuinness,' *The Crows Behind the Plough: History and Violence in Anglo-Irish Poetry and Drama*, ed. Geert Lernout (Amsterdam: Coster, 1991), p.100.

6 Anthony Roche concludes his discussion of McGuinness by identifying him as 'the true son of Sam'. Anthony Roche, *Contemporary Irish Drama from Beckett to McGuinness* (New York: St. Martin's Press, 1995), p.278.

7 Frank McGuinness, *Innocence* (London: Faber and Faber, 1987), p.3; hereafter cited parenthetically thus: (*I* 3).

8 Frank McGuinness, 'Personal Concerns,' interview with Colm O'Briain, Radio Telefís Éireann, cited in Eamonn Jordan, *The Feast of Famine*. (Bern: Peter Lang, 1997).

9 Frank McGuinness, *Baglady*, in *Carthaginians* and *Baglady* (London: Faber and Faber, 1987), p.75; hereafter cited parenthetically, thus: (*B* 75).

10 Frank McGuinness, 'Personal Concerns'.

11 Frank McGuinness, *Observe the Sons of Ulster Marching Towards the Somme* (London: Faber and Faber, 1986), p.57; hereafter cited parenthetically, thus: (*OSU* 57).

12 James Joyce, *Ulysses*, ed. Hans Walter Gabler (New York: Vintage, 19867), p.34. Terence Brown argues that 'In both the Nationalist and Unionist versions of the Irish past there is therefore a profound sense of history as a given, as a nightmare from which it is impossible to awake.' Terence Brown, *Ireland's Literature: Selected Essays* (Totowa, NJ: Barnes and Noble, 1988), p.245.

13 Frank McGuinness, 'Alone Again, Naturally,' interview with John Waters, *In Dublin*, (14 May 1987), p.16.

14 While researching *Observe the Sons of Ulster*, McGuinness 'was quite overwhelmed by the diversity within the Protestant mind through the whole island, but concentrated, as it is, in the North'. McGuinness, 'Personal Concerns'.

15 'Frank McGuinness: A Profile'.

16 Frank McGuinness, *Carthaginians*, in *Carthaginians* and *Baglady* (London: Faber and Faber, 1987), p.24; hereafter cited parenthetically, thus: (*C* 24).

17 'I am attracted', McGuinness has said, 'to those fighting desperate odds'. Frank McGuinness, 'An Irishman's Theatre', in *Studies in Contemporary Irish Theatre: Actes du Colloque de Caen*, ed. Jacqueline Genet (Caen: Caen Press Université, 1991), p.61.

18 For a discussion of the linkage of Derry and Carthage, see Elizabeth Butler Cullingford, 'British Romans and Irish Carthaginians:

Anti-colonial Metaphor in Heaney, Friel, and McGuinness, *PMLA*, 111(1996), pp.222-39.
[19] William Shakespeare, *The Complete Works*, ed. David Bevington, 4th ed. (New York: Harper, 1992), 1.2.42.
[20] For a discussion of the ambiguities of gender in *Carthaginians*, see Elizabeth Butler Cullingford, 'Gender, Sexuality, and Englishness in Modern Irish Drama and Film', in *Gender and Sexuality in Modern Ireland*, ed. Anthony Bradley, Maryann Gialanella Valiulis (Amherst: University of Massachusetts Press, 1997), pp.159-86.
[21] Christopher Murray, *Twentieth-Century Irish Drama: Mirror Up to Nation* (New York: St. Martin's Press, 1997), p.207.
[22] In *Someone Who'll Watch Over Me*, Adam is not perforce an African American. He was played by a black actor in the first New York and London productions of the play, but by a white actor in the Abbey Theatre premiere. McGuinness has said that he did not create Adam as a black character, Frank McGuinness, interview with the author.
[23] Specifically referring to the prisoners in Nazi concentration camps, Viktor Frankl asserts that 'Man does not simply exist but always decides what his existence will be'. Viktor Frankl, *Man's Search for Meaning*, trans. Ilse Lasch (New York: Simon and Schuster, 1959), p.133. Frankl's work and writings are particularly germane to *Observe the Sons of Ulster*, for the play's 'Pairing' section –and especially Millen's coaching Moore to cross the bridge and thereby overcome his greatest fear –recalls Frankl's therapeutic methods.
[24] Frank McGuinness, *Someone Who'll Watch Over Me* (London: Faber and Faber, 1992), pp.23-24; hereafter cited parenthetically, thus: (*S* 23-24).
[25] Albert Camus, 'The Myth of Sisyphus', in *The Myth of Sisyphus and Other Essays*, trans. Justin O'Brien (New York: Vintage, 1960), p.108.

Of *Mutabilitie*
Christopher Murray

1.

In many of his plays, excluding perhaps *The Factory Girls*, McGuinness likes to introduce and deconstruct stereotypes. The method is often transgressive and may involve a kind of Lord of the Revels figure who ratifies the transgression. This figure is a catalyst, a someone not only to watch over the weak or the imprisoned or the vulnerable but to goad or to inspire the timid and the confused towards self-realization and change.

Examples would range from Dido in *Carthaginians* to Rima in *Dolly West's Kitchen*. At other times there is no discernible agent of change, which, defying Beckett's drama, derives from the situation and the friction between characters. But even in such cases McGuinness imagines in Shakespearean vein a mysterious force in history which transcends the horrors of war or misery in order to bring about a wished-for end. I would say 'Shakespearean' broadly in the sense of the romances or final plays, from *Pericles* to *The Tempest* and *Henry VIII*, where time and providence seem magically to intertwine and where the gods, the godlike and the king 'watch over' the fallible characters in their blundering voyages towards self-discovery. But the early history plays, as will appear, also underpin McGuinness's *oeuvre*.

Mutabilitie observes and carries through this heuristic design in highly complex ways. The play is rich in ideas and themes, so rich, I would maintain, that it finally collapses under the impossible burden and, to borrow a line from *Hamlet*, 'growing to a plurisy,/ Dies in [its] own too much' (Norton 1738). Well, not quite dies. *Mutabilitie* remains an important play in McGuinness's *oeuvre* because it works out in greater detail than ever before his fascination with stereotypes (national, gender-based, theatrical) and with the drama of necessary transformation and transcendence.

For the purposes of this essay I want to focus on *Mutabilitie* as an Irish history play. Here it has two contexts, the Shakespearean and the contemporary Irish scene, political as well as dramatic. The history play was virtually Shakespeare's invention, although Marlowe was a significant trailblazer. For McGuinness, *Richard II* is a key text. This was a play he came to know intimately when as a graduate student he played Bolingbroke in Joseph Long's production at University College Dublin in 1976. He was a magnificent Bolingbroke, all fire and air, a man of destiny come to sweep aside the effeminate king. The text has remained with him as a reference point: even when speaking on *The Tempest* at the Abbey Theatre (14 December 1999), where a postcolonialist production was running, McGuinness invoked *Richard II* as a powerful prior example of self-construction and self-knowledge.[1] In his own plays it is the deposed or captive or player king who receives McGuinness's main attention. Whether consciously or not, he worked through Yeats's idea of *Richard II*, in which Yeats inverted the conventional English celebration of the man of action (Bolingbroke) and elevated in his place Richard's frailty as artistic strength:

> I have turned over many books in the library at Stratford-on-Avon, and I have found in nearly all an antithesis, which grew in clearness and violence as the [nineteenth] century grew older, between two types, whose representatives were Richard II, 'sentimental', 'weak', 'selfish', 'insincere', and Henry V, 'Shakespeare's only hero.' These books took the same delight in abasing Richard II that schoolboys do in persecuting some boy of fine temperament, who has weak muscles and a distaste for school games. (Yeats, 103-04)

Yeats clearly genders the argument here, though stopping short of 'queering' it. His case, elaborated with care, makes one see how Shaw could have based Marchbanks in *Candida* on Yeats: the paradox is that the weaker emerges as the stronger in the tussle between two stereotypes. Yeats, no doubt, in some measure identified with Richard II, to whom he deliberately gave 'Celtic' credentials in defiance of Edward Dowden.

Yeats made Henry V rather than Bolingbroke ('any common man', Yeats 106) the antithesis of Richard's aesthetic decadence. Shakespeare's *Henry V* is a key text in any inspection of Irish-English relations, even though its plot concerns the wars in France. So familiar now is the exchange in 3.3 between Captain Macmorris (the first stage Irishman) and Fluellen (a stage Welshman) that its political edge may perhaps be blunted but can never fail to ignite the Anglo-Irish debate:

> **Fluellen:** Captain MacMorris, I think, look you, under your correction, there is not many of your nation –
> **Macmorris:** Of my nation? What ish my nation? Ish a villain and a bastard and a knave and a rascal? What ish my nation? Who talks of my nation? (Norton 1479)

MacMorris's question, even if ironic, is still the central one in postcolonial Ireland. It energizes much of Heaney's poetry, from *North* to *Station Island*. It is quoted direct in McGuinness's *Mutabilitie*, but significantly, perversely, it is Spenser the colonizer who puts the question and not any of the colonized, and it is Shakespeare who answers:

> **William:** Your powers are very great.
> **Edmund:** As my nation is great. What is my nation?
> **William:** England. (51)

The certainty of the reply gives notice that William can have nothing in common with the native Irish. Shaman though he is, avatar even, this Shakespeare is not about to undertake the burden of Irish history. A passage from Philip Edwards's important essay is à propos (236): 'The tone of much of the writing about Shakespeare and Ireland in recent years has been accusatory and contemptuous. Shakespeare has been tried in his absence, and convicted of sharing in the racist denigration which lubricated the ruthless programme of conquest, suppression and occupation.' In McGuinness's play, however, Shakespeare is present for his trial and exposure.

In one sense, *Mutabilitie* seeks to rewrite *Henry V* by using Spenser as the bad conscience of imperialism. In the chorus introducing Act 5 Shakespeare hunts for comparisons to vivify Henry's triumphant return from France. Conquering Caesar is an obvious start. Then follows the Earl of Essex, mistakenly assumed to be about to return from Ireland in glory, wrenched from the defeat of Hugh O'Neill:

> As, by a lower but high-loving likelihood,
> Were now the General of our gracious Empress [*sic*]—
> As in good time he may -- from Ireland coming,
> Bringing rebellion broached on his sword,
> How many would the peaceful city quit
> To welcome him! Much more, and much more cause,
> Did they this Harry. (Norton 1511)

Essex left London for Ireland in March 1599; by September his campaign was in ruins, and recalled in ignominy by Elizabeth Essex soon turned rebel himself.[2] Though Shakespeare had got it wrong in predicting (as he wrote his *Henry V*) that a contemporary hero would 'in good time' vindicate a simile, the error stands also as a vindication of mutability. What seems certain can suddenly dissolve into uncertainty. From the Irish perspective Hugh O'Neill was the hero likely to deliver Ireland from English oppression. But he too was destined to fail and with his failure condemn the Irish to long-term colonization (in contrast to Henry's short-term victory admitted in the epilogue to *Henry V*). Both Thomas Kilroy and Brian Friel have dramatized O'Neill's tragic failure, the one in *The O'Neill* (1969), the other in *Making History* (1988). McGuinness avoids this tragic scenario and opts instead for a clash of equal but different cultures whose reconciliation can never successfully be achieved through violence, whether imperialist or revolutionary.

2.

Mutabilitie is a play which, in the guise of a story of Spenser's failed attempt to impose civilization on what he saw as a barbaric people, recommends a solution to a racial conflict with its roots in colonialism. The opening lines of the play not only address the issue of imperialism but of national identity: Spenser speaks to the stranger William, 'I am an Englishman. I am Edmund. Despite your ragged clothing I know you are a civilized man' (3). 'Civilized', that is, in contrast with the barbaric Irish. Edmund later quotes from his own prose text, *A View of the Present State of Ireland,* which supports violence against the uncivilized Irish. Yet the play introduces us to a Spenser who is in crisis. He has written his great national epic, *The Faerie Queene,* and now seems in mental turmoil because the native population has suffered too much. He is, in fact, going mad as a result of his guilt. He is the artist for whom political necessity has proved less tolerable in practice than in theory. Eventually he burns down his own castle, which is McGuinness's invention. On the contrary, it was the native Irish who burned Spenser and his family out, causing the death in the fire of one of his children. By changing the facts, McGuinness can show Spenser as a guilty representative of colonialist oppression (or, indeed, as a typical Anglo-Irish landlord).

On the other hand, *Mutabilitie* is a play about two rival but equal cultures. The dispossessed Irish are represented as anthropologically and artistically sophisticated. They are not primitive; they are merely different: the postcolonial argument is strongly asserted. They have their poet, called File, just as the English have theirs, called Spenser. It seems not to have been noticed that in creating the Gaelic poet as a woman McGuinness was outrageously defying a patriarchal tradition in the ancient Irish academy. [Gaelic poets were officially male.] The effect is to introduce a possibility which conflicts with what otherwise stands as unalterable history. As McGuinness sees it, though he is no Marxist, all is amorphous and amenable to change. (One may bring to mind here his adaptation of *The*

Threepenny Opera, Gate Theatre, in July 1991, which posed the question, 'What if Brecht and O'Casey, in a dream, wandered through Dublin?'³). In this alienating and destabilizing manner McGuinness also gives the Irish king and queen (counterpart of Elizabeth) the names Sweney and Maeve, echoes of Irish mythological characters. Ireland had no king in the sixteenth century: indeed the last high king reigned in the twelfth century, after which petty kings feuded for a time until leaders of septs and clans no longer invoked the name. McGuinness places Sweney and Maeve into the aftermath of the Munster plantation to underline the displacement and the madness it occasioned. He introduces them as ruined remnants of a broken aristocracy, whose failure demands execution within the tribe. In turn, execution breeds unappeasable guilt, and it is this guilt which forms a thematic bond with Spenser's collapse and self-destruction.

McGuinness renders Spenser as sympathetic as Shakespeare did Richard II: a move which counteracts Yeats's famous denigration of Spenser and allows an alliance between the two sensibilities divided in time by two centuries. Yeats could not disguise his disgust at Spenser's turning art to imperialistic purposes. He saw Spenser as 'the first salaried moralist among the poets' (369), and commented further: 'When Spenser wrote of Ireland he wrote as an official, and out of thoughts and emotions that had been organized by the State. He was the first of many Englishmen to see nothing but what he was desired to see' (372). In Yeats's view Spenser, who might have learned to perfect his art by acquiring a Celtic folk-culture, had missed a great opportunity. While McGuinness does not deny this – indeed, the idea is taken for granted – he pushes forward past Yeatsian condemnation into the possibility of seeing Spenser's failure as the seed of a new growth (ultimately to produce a truly Anglo-Irish literary ascendancy). Yet Shakespeare's Richard II, the key mediating figure in this cultural debate, had a contemporary resonance in the late Elizabethan age. For in banning a revival of Shakespeare's play during Essex's rebellion Elizabeth is reported to have identified with the threatened sensitive monarch: 'I am Richard II. Know ye not that?' (Ure lix).

By imaginatively reconfiguring history and real literary figures McGuinness works towards his resolution through communion. There was nothing new here: He had resolved *Carthaginians* and *Someone Who'll Watch Over Me* similarly. In the latter play the Englishman Michael breaks through the Irishman Edward's despair by reciting George Herbert's seventeenth-century poem 'Love': love is personified, greets the sinful soul and draws him into the hospitality of the dining-room. Love is Christ, who says finally to the guilt-filled guest, 'You must sit down ... and taste my meat', and the poem ends in the soul's acceptance: 'So I did sit and eat' (*Someone* 41). As *Mutabilitie* draws to a close, following Spenser's mad attack on his own castle, and the violence self-inflicted by the Irish, Spenser's young son wanders lost into the Irish camp. The Irish adopt him. 'He is to be fostered as our own. Reared as our own. Nurtured like our own, and natured like *his* own' (100-01, emphasis added). The child is to share in both Irish and English traditions. The child being hungry the Irish poet File gives him milk to drink and commands him to eat. The last line of the play, a stage direction, echoes Herbert's poem: '*They sit and eat. Music*' (101).

As Hiroko Mikami has shown in detail (108-26), *Mutabilitie*, in its metamorphosis of Irish and English opponents and stereotypes, was shaped as a metaphor for the Belfast Agreement evolving while the play ran at the Royal National Theatre from November 1998 (Mikami 113). McGuinness has more than once allowed his art thus to intervene directly in the Irish-English debate. Of *Observe the Sons of Ulster* it has recently been said: 'Written in the wake of a hostile unionist reaction to the New Ireland Forum, McGuinness's play was an attempt to engage positively with the loyalist ideology of Ulster Protestantism.' Performed in 1985, it coincided with the Anglo-Irish Agreement which 'conceded that Ireland should have a consultative role in the government of Northern Ireland' (Pilkington 221, 223). There is something discomfiting about this proximity between art and politics. But if there is, there is also a daring altogether characteristic. Moreover if *Mutabilitie*, like *Observe the Sons of Ulster*, in some measure demonstrates 'ideological conformity to the political interests of the state', is this more or less than Spenser did in *The Faerie Queene*? Further, even if it be agreed that McGuinness's plays, like many Irish plays, sometimes attempt this ideological strategy, 'this is a conformity that seldom neutralizes or exhausts the theatre's subversive potential' (Pilkington 223).

3.

Mutabilitie encompasses this subversive tradition which gives theatre its continuing energy. It is a fact that before colonization began in the twelfth century Ireland had no native theatrical tradition. There is therefore a huge paradox inherent in the idea of a nationalist Irish theatre – as founded in 1899 by Yeats, Lady Gregory, and Edward Martyn – dedicated to putting on stage the history and reality of Irish experience in an occupied country. From the 1660s on, 'there was no mistaking the link between the [Dublin] theatre and sound monarchist views, and the stage beckoned as an avenue of political rehabilitation' (Morash 12). Irish theatre, historically, was thus a colonialist Anglo-Irish cultural formation, exclusive in many ways. The nationalist reaction, while indebted to this tradition for the structures set in place, had no alternative but to revolt. It was as we find in *The Tempest*: Caliban accepts the fact that he learned English from the daughter of his colonial master, 'and my profit on't / Is I know how to curse' (Norton 3066). In *Mutabilitie* McGuinness acknowledges this heritage not without irony (given that his play had its premiere in London's Royal National Theatre). The Irish poet (File) addressing the English (Shakespeare) asks about the alien art of theatre: 'Is it not now a sacred dwelling? Is it not a temple where the remembered dead rise from their graves?' (56). Such an ideal hardly matched the rough, subversive Elizabethan professional playhouse, always under moral supervision and reprehension. But when William conjures up the play-within-the-play about the Trojan War, it is paradoxically shown how magic and miracle can reverse things and create life anew. This, in a way, was to be the Yeatsian project. In *Mutabilitie* McGuinness wishes to create a play assimilating all of the history of colonialism in Ireland and yet by resurrecting it find within it a basis for what the File calls 'reformation' (56).

4.

Spenser's 'The Mutability Cantos', which gave title and major theme to McGuinness's play, remained unfinished. The central idea is a debate or *agon* on change, whether nature or 'mutability' holds primacy in the universe. No poet, perhaps, held a more profound sense of change than did Spenser:

> What Man that sees the ever-whirling wheele
> Of *Change*, the which all mortall things doth sway,
> But that thereby doth find & plainly feele,
> How MUTABILITY in them doth play
> Her cruell sports, to many mens decay? . . . (Spenser 1025)

Change was 'great *Chaos* child' (1032), claiming unjust dispossession of heavenly rights. In short, Mutabilitie, as Titaness, challenged Jove's supremacy. She was thus a rebel, as Ireland was a rebel, against the imperium of the natural course of things. Hence Nature herself is invoked to adjudicate the argument between Mutabilitie and Jove. In the political reading of the Cantos, Mutabilitie is Ireland, Nature is Queen Elizabeth (Hadfield 189). The only way Nature can decide is by arguing that change is not decay but a natural form of perfectibility (Spenser 1054). Elsewhere Spenser saw this drama in the more familiar terms of art versus nature.

It was a commonplace medieval and Renaissance idea that everything sublunary was subject to change. To the poets of the Elizabethan period this fact was a cause for grief and a theme for elegizing the decay of beauty: Shakespeare's sonnets sing of little else. But Spenser looked further and saw art as transcending change, transforming nature into a freeze-frame of eternal beauty. Thus in the Garden of Adonis (in Book 3, canto 6, of *The Faerie Queene*) the poet's imagined paradise, Spenser constructs the paradox of beauty 'eterne in mutabilitie' (Spenser 473), beauty held in suspense through the power of the imagination. Nature is transcended but not denied. Energy infuses all with unifying force. While the second law of thermodynamics may nowadays hold such a notion up to question poetry/art can nevertheless persist in wishful thinking, taking its cue from Shaw's Serpent in *Back to Methuselah*: 'I dream things that never were; and I say 'Why not?' I made the word dead to describe my old skin that I cast when I am renewed. I call that renewal being born' (Shaw II, 7). In his own day Spenser might have found the idea articulated in Sidney's *A Defence of Poetry* (1595), where Sidney sees the poet/artist as capable of achieving a perfection nature (or reality) leaves unfinished. 'Nature never set forth the earth in so rich tapestry as divers poets have done; neither with so pleasant rivers, fruitful trees, sweet-smelling flowers, nor whatsoever else may make the too much loved earth more lovely. Her world is brazen [made of mere brass], the poets only deliver a golden.' (Sidney 24). The idealizing power of the imagination, here romantically conceived, was to enter the Anglo-Irish tradition with Edmund Burke and reach its apogee in Yeats (see 'Sailing to Byzantium' for example), and against this tradition McGuinness's art must be defined.

McGuinness skilfully assimilates Spenser's two quite different notions of mutability, the one in the unfinished 'Mutability Cantos' (or book 7 of *The Faerie Queene*) and the other from the central Book 3 of the poem, the narrative, proper. By combining the two concepts and fitting them into a dramatization of political conflict and its imagined resolution outside of time, McGuinness attempts something extraordinarily difficult. Where Spenser can see only God as the ultimate converter of mutability into changelessness, into Himself (Spenser 1055), McGuinness makes Spenser as character party to a wordly historical pageant of transformation. Compared to Friel, in particular, among those modern Irish playwrights who have looked to the late sixteenth century as image of contemporary political circumstance, McGuinness is an optimist: he believes in rebirth, situations capable of regeneration.[4] Friel, for his part, dwells upon what might have been, the triumph of mutability.

The elegiac note closes *Making History* as it does so many of Friel's plays, with battles lost and wholeness blasted. For McGuinness drama is a ritual of healing. Mutability is all for the best in the end.

Mutabilitie, then, sees change as positive, sees Irish-English relations as capable of renaissance. There is, in some measure, a high emotionalism about such a vision. It is not a logical or Shavian dramatic idea. Far from being dialectical, McGuinness writes organically, scene upon scene, theme upon theme. There is a burgeoning of material, or character interaction, marked by a fierce expenditure of energy in the romantic mode. There is in his work usually no clear through-line of dramatic action. In its place persists a Blakean neglect of the logic of plot development in favour of scenes autonomously existent and emotionally viable: discrete, intense, polarized, lyrical. McGuinness introduces stereoypes, national and/or gendered, to provide for their transformation within a new emerging situation, tragic in *Observe the Sons of Ulster,* positive and forward-looking in *Someone Who'll Watch Over Me* (a pivotal text) and in both *Mutabilitie* and *Dolly West's Kitchen.* This transformation is, perhaps necessarily, politically inflected but fundamentally it embodies a dynamic which generates images of a new beginning: mutability in action, its end peace.

[1] Even in *Gates of Gold,* McGuinness's recent play about a dying actor (Gate Theatre, Dublin, 30 April-8 June 2002), *Richard II* is subtly encoded. The actor quotes the opening of John of Gaunt's dying speech, a role he never actually played but had hoped to graduate to from the flamboyant Richard. In the context, the prophecy of national scandal is merely ludic as no devastation awaits the nation (here Ireland rather than England) following the death of this actor, Gabriel.

[2] For a discussion of Shakespeare's use of similes for the triumphant Henry V, see Gary Taylor, ed., *Henry V* (Oxford: OUP, 1984), p.12.

[3] Frank McGuinness, 'Dreams' programme note for *The Threepenny Opera,* by Bertolt Brecht, a version by Frank McGuinness, Gate Theatre, Dublin, July-August 1991.

[4] *Gates of Gold*, starkly focused on death, may seem to prove the exception. But even here McGuinness creates transcendence by an emphasis on Gabriel's death as, in a word, triumphant.

Works Cited

Edwards, Philip, 'Shakespeare, Ireland, Dreamland,' *Irish University Review* 28.2 (1998), pp.227-39.

Hadfield, Andrew, *Edmund Spenser's Irish Experience: Wilde Fruit and Salvage Soyle* (Oxford: Clarendon Press, 1997).

McGuinness, Frank, *Someone Who'll Watch Over Me* (London and Boston: Faber and Faber, 1992).

――― *Mutabilitie* (London and Boston: Faber and Faber, 1997). *Gates of Gold* (London and Boston: Faber and Faber, 2002).

Mikami, Hiroko, *Frank McGuinness and his Theatre of Paradox* (Gerrards Cross: Colin Smythe, 2002).

Morash, Christopher, *A History of Irish Theatre* (Cambridge: University Press, 2002).

[Norton] Shakespeare, William, *The Norton Shakespeare: Based on the Oxford Edition*, ed. Stephen Greenblatt et al (New York and London: W.W. Norton, 1997).

Pilkington, Lionel, *Theatre and the State in Twentieth-Century Ireland: Cultivating the People* (London and New York: Routledge, 2001).

Sidney, Sir Philip, *A Defence of Poetry*, ed. Jan Van Dorsten (Oxford: Oxford University Press, 1973).

Spenser, Edmund, *The Faerie Queene*, ed. Thomas P. Roche Jr (Harmonsworth: Penguin, 1978).

Shaw, Bernard, *Complete Plays with Prefaces* (6 vols., New York: Dodd, Mead, 1963).

Taylor, Gary, ed. *William Shakespeare, Henry V* (Oxford: OUP, 1984).

Ure, Peter, ed., *King Richard II*, Arden Edition of the Works of William Shakespeare (London and New York: Methuen, 1961).

Yeats, W.B., *Essays and Introductions* (London and New York: Macmillan, 1961).

A Director's Perspective on *Mutabilitie*
Michael Caven in conversation with Helen Lojek

[**Michael Caven** is Artistic Director of The Theatreworks Company (Dublin). He was nominated for an Irish Times/ESB Best Director Award in 1999 (for *Anna Karenina*) and in 2001 (for *Richard III*). In 2000 he directed the Irish premiere of *Mutabilitie* at the Samuel Beckett Theatre (Trinity College, Dublin). Sinéad Cuthbert won an Irish Times/ESB Award for Best Costume Design for the production, and Paul Keogan was nominated for a Best Lighting Design award. Caven spoke by telephone with Helen Lojek in May 2002.]

HL: What led to your production of Mutabilitie?

MC: Nine months or a year before the Royal National Theatre production [directed by Trevor Nunn at London's Cottesloe Theatre in 1997] I was lucky enough to read a copy of the script. On Frank's original draft the first few words were something like 'A forest. A heath. A castle. A river. Earth. Air. Water. Fire'; there followed an extraordinarily short scene in which figures run through a forest as the drums roll as other dark figures of menace drop from the trees. Then the words 'God save us! Jesus save us! William save us!' A shiver went up my spine. Those words completely stopped me in my tracks. 'William save us!' Shakespeare comes to Ireland – and he can save us! The power of that first scene and those that tumbled by after it sparked off something that utterly fascinates me – Renaissance metaphysics and theatre of memory. As I got fuller and fuller into this extraordinarily dense world that Frank had produced I realized I was in the presence of what I now regard as a truly great play.

It is so monumental that in many ways the age we live in is not ready for it. Like all great works it harks back to something and yet also looks forward to a refreshing revival of a theatre that springs fully from the imagination. The intellect at work in it is there to produce an imaginative, poetic, inner explosion in the watcher rather than a psychological, logical progression through a recognizable Freudian world. It's a great sweeping masque of a play reminding me of *The Tempest* and of plays such as *Life is a Dream* by [seventeenth century Spanish playwright] Calderon and even *Camino Real* by Tennessee Williams. A totally brave, ambitious play that breaks every contemporary rule of what a play is supposed to be about. Although it took a lot of reading and re-reading to sift all the layers from its dense depths, I found it easily digestible as the language and subject matter were very close to my heart, particularly its politics, its historical mischief making and its theatrical spirituality. I desperately wanted to do it.

At that stage it was quite clearly out of the question, because it was going into rehearsal at the RNT as a joint production between the two national theatres of England and Ireland, and was then due to come back to Dublin after its opening in London. In these circumstances a production in Ireland directed by me was just not going to happen. I then went along to a rehearsed reading, directed by Patrick Mason and performed by members of the Abbey Company, interestingly enough, during a Shakespeare conference in Trinity College. Listening to it had another overwhelming impact on me and the desire to stage it burned ever stronger. Still, I wished Frank and the production great success in England, knowing that the chances of me directing it were minute unless it was at some time in the distant future. And yet something in me told me this was not to be the end of the story. I didn't anticipate what was to take place. The London production met with mixed reviews, and the decision was taken not to bring the production back to Ireland. The play from an Irish point of view went dead.

Time went by, but the desire to do the play didn't go away. I contacted Frank about six months after the London production closed. He said he appreciated my interest, but that at that juncture he wasn't ready to see the piece produced again. He wanted time for the dust to settle. I felt strongly that an Irish production was vital, that this great work should not sit neglected on the shelf. So, a year later I again wrote to him. One day soon after, I came home to find a message on my answering machine, brief and to the point: 'This is Frank. You can do it.' Having been given permission it was then a question of trying to mount a production that would do the piece justice with the limited resources at the disposal of such a small independent company. I knew I wanted to do the piece at the Samuel Beckett Theatre in Trinity; when Trevor Nunn wrote to say he couldn't come to see our production, he said he was delighted to see it was going on in the Samuel Beckett, because that's where he'd intended doing it [if the RNT production had come to Dublin]. My company, Theatreworks, produces all its work there, and we have a passionate relationship to that space. I knew that the correct use of space was key to releasing the play's potential. This extraordinary story takes place in a non-realistic, very poetic, magical landscape. The Beckett Theatre is not the biggest theatre in the world in terms of capacity (circa 250), but does have a tremendously powerful stage (It's about 50 or 60 feet high, 50 or so feet wide and about the same deep - a great cathedral of a place) and a great relationship to an audience. I knew I was going to use that whole stage so that this vast story could have a vast theatrical landscape. So the decision was taken to go ahead and I began to put the production together.

HL: *From the start what you see as the imaginative, non-realistic world of the play determined the staging?*

MC: I find it hard to describe, but I start from a visceral feeling, an imaginative vision in space. Words make me see images, movements, groupings, and sounds, in space. I'm hugely influenced by classic, Renaissance spatial imagination. I call myself a radical classicist, and I work in terms of the landscape of that world at all times. I see words in three-dimensional pictures – very deep and broad and full of colour. I've been heavily influenced by all the great high Renaissance painters and architects, particularly the religious images and spaces they produced. Cathedrals. Large civic buildings. Temples. Squares. Groupings of bodies within these spaces. They somehow all seem to have got into my blood ever since I was a child, and whenever I think of a piece of theatre I tend to see it in a very architectural scale, in a heightened scale, not in a realistic or every day scale. I'm also heavily influenced by the great Renaissance hermetic thinkers such as Robert Fludd and of course Shakespeare himself, who saw the theatre as a place where the imagination of tribe, of memory, of the soul could be brought to transubstantive life through movements based on geometric patterns. They believed that the theatre used in this manner affects people powerfully, gets under the skin, gets into that place in the imagination that cannot be quantified and qualified. Theatre that teaches us to understand by fully *apprehending* rather than merely *comprehending*. This too is my faith.

HL: *Your vision of theatre is also, it seems to me, the vision in* Mutabilitie, *which is more large scale than many other McGuinness works, but also more large scale than many other Irish plays. Do you have a preference for large-scale productions?*

MC: Yes. My reputation is based on large-scale productions. People think of me as the maker of the 'big play.' My most recent production was *Richard III*. I am fascinated by big stories of sweep and scale that pass through time and space. My guru is Shakespeare. I grew up obsessed by his works, and that obsession has never left me. Any Shakespeare play breaks all the great rules of time and space. You go through time; you go through space; you journey from environment to environment. Time is something that gallops or trots or races. The only thing that stops you is the boundaries of your own imagination. I think that theatre at the moment is suffering from an over-propensity to intellectualize in a truly rational sense, rather than to remember that its greatest power is as a visceral, imaginative force. A force that is *not* like the rest of the world. It's about finding a way of showing the unseen. I think you're right. Irish theatre tends to be quite domestic, and to be oriented towards the small scale. The family and the personal are at the heart of a lot of Irish writing. But Frank wants to write about 'Otherness'. All his plays are centred on something or someone that propels the story out of narrow boundaries, out of the boundaries of Ireland, off into other horizons, both of nationality, of time, space, and of imagination. His work is constantly transcendent, even something like *Someone Who'll Watch Over Me* that appears to be an intimate piece about men trapped in a small room. Yet there are moments when it flies. And flying is a hugely important part of great theatre. A leap of faith. A leap of vision. All of Frank's plays at some point, and some at many points, are constantly trying to take off, into a different dimension of experience that we just do not find on the surface. *Mutabilitie* is like that from beginning to end. It never for one second tries to pretend to be anything other than a huge *theatrical* experience, a Mass in a sense. Every scene is trying to use Frank's belief in the transformative, transcendent power of theatre to make people shift internally, to experience a thought or a feeling about themselves as individuals, about their imaginations, about their sense of Irishness or Englishness or whatever, that is not out of a pamphlet or out of a dogma or out of a textbook, but something that comes at them from out of the mist or out of the wind in the trees or out of the roughness of the earth.

HL: *Given the emphasis on the mystical power of this play, as well as the tendency of audiences to go for a rational, naturalistic explanation, what knowledge of history do you think an audience needs to understand this play?*

MC: That's a very important question. It's a hard one. We obviously came up against it in rehearsal. I confess we did a lot of work in the early days of rehearsal to assimilate the historical background. Not a lot of people are up to speed on sixteenth century imperial English power in Ireland or the relationship of Edmund Spenser to his poetry and to his role as a civil servant – or what was going on in sixteenth century Ireland and England. Yet the actors needed to digest this information or they couldn't begin to play it. However, what an actor needs to know to perform and what an audience needs to watch are not the same thing. All actors of worth recognize that research is vital to setting off the creative juices; that in some senses they must end up knowing more about the character and his/her environment/history than the character does. But you can kill an audience dead in their seats if you start producing theatre as academic lecture. So we had to decide, do we need to put great big notes in the program for the audience about the politics of the time; do we need to put stuff in the foyer with pictures and diagrams and all of that? We decided to avoid this as much as possible, because I felt that we had to trust our audience and not lead them down any cul-de-sac. Those who got most out of the play said that they knew they could have got lost if they'd let themselves become obsessed in the moment of watching with trying to work it out. What they chose to do instead was to immerse themselves in the production and go with it, bask in its fullness, come out afterwards and feel what they felt and find from it what they found. Bits would evade everybody, but it was extraordinary how many understood it even though they did not know the facts, figures, and dates that the play alludes to.

Those who completely resisted the play were obsessed with the superficial reality of a historical world or pedantic issues of literary structuring: 'There was no way William Shakespeare came to Ireland…and after all Edmund Spenser blah, blah, blah…and how can you put him side by side with mythical figures such as King Sweney and Maeve, bla, bla, bla!' They rationalized themselves into a dead end. Several critics were vicious about the structure of the play, claiming that it was no play at all; that it tried to do too much and failed to deliver any form of clarity. For me the play overwhelmed the limits of their theatrical imagination and it was easier for them to try and bury it than deal with its fullness. By keeping historical notes out of the program, I wanted to free people to simply encounter the play in performance. I believe passionately in audiences. I know there's a huge debate going on about the dumbing-down of culture, of which there is much truth. Yet, as a creative force the theatre fails too often to truly engage an audience in a manner that allows them to be a good audience. I believe that if you reach out, if you put integrity and creative force into something and reach out to the audience, saying 'Share this with us', rather than saying 'Keep away', people will come and experience it. That great phrase, 'If you build it, they will come.' Yes, we had people walk out at the interval of every performance, but not because they were bored, not because they didn't care, but because the play had such a powerful impact on them that they had to resist it, they had to hate it, or they had to be angry about it, or they had to flee it, particularly after say the great choral scene that closes the first half. It didn't bother me. We were doing our job when we got that reaction. If a piece of theatre does not explode upon an audience, does not shake our complacency, does not stir us, I do not see the point of it. *Mutabilitie* is a play that should come at you like a multi-coloured roller coaster and wash over you and throw you out the other end of the theatre, breathless and not quite sure what happened – like a great piece of music – but absolutely stirred by it, and desperate to hear that sound again and again.

HL: *Some critics have described* Mutabilitie *as a play that is 'too focused on language.' Your production included wonderful spectacle as well. What sort of balance were you seeking?*

MC: I don't agree for one moment that the play is focused on language – it is focused on using powerful language to create powerful, visual drama. I believe, as Hamlet says, you should 'suit the action to the word ...' Every word is energy in movement. Every line delivered is in some kind of motion. When I read a text, consider language, I'm always thinking of movement through the actors' bodies, movement through sound, movement through lighting and through space.

In terms of what you call spectacle, I knew the first time I read the play that it *must not* be done naturalistically. I didn't see the London production and don't want to say too much about it, but I believe that one of the problems was probably the decision to create a very physically realistic world that was built out of objects that were tangible and said very loudly, 'Look I am a river and me, I'm a castle!' I believe you have to think carefully about the visual language by which you choose to communicate with an audience. If you visually suggest that this is a real place, i.e. a place of surface, they will then expect a play that takes place on or close to that surface. If you put a play that's so essentially about the unseen into a concrete world, the contradictions can cause huge cracks to appear in an audience's willingness to suspend disbelief. What I wanted to do was to manipulate the total flexibility of space offered by the Beckett Theatre, creating (primarily through height and depth) different places and shifts in time and place that would enable the drama to continually evolve but not lock it into a surface dimension. From this came the decision to build a neutrally defined and yet dynamically shaped structure that represented the castle. The same went for the forest and the river, both of which were principally created by light defining open space. This meant the audience were told to use their imaginations. This I have found is something audiences love you for. If you show them everything they say 'I don't have to work, so I'll fall asleep. It's a building, and there it is, yes there're bricks on the front of it.' But if you say 'This could be a building but could also turn into a tree', they suddenly say 'Ah, thank you. I'm a child again. I am here to play.'

Using height was very important. Within Frank's play there is the sense of the earth, the sense of the high sky, the sense of the air in between. I wanted to create that Renaissance concept of the above, the middle, and below. People were watching, people were moving on a height – travelling up, travelling down. Light played a fundamental part in creating and defining the imaginative boundaries of those various spaces. Light you can change in a second. In a play like *Mutabilitie* you have to pick a modern audience up and hold it in a vice-like grip, so that they feel confident and comfortable in the world you are showing them. Scene changes that involve a lot of mechanics slow down the movement and can be fatal. The rational mind kicks back in and resists what the imagination is saying.

HL: *I'm particularly interested in the use of space in the scene in Act Three, where there is a split stage and overlapping dialogue – somewhat like the split stage in* Observe the Sons of Ulster, *but this time with some gender contrasts as well.*

MC: I'll never forget that when the company finished their first reading of that scene, they spontaneously gave themselves a great big round of applause – as if they knew they were facing an acting tunnel of almost unprecedented terror. It's something like nine pages of one-line cues spoken by 12 actors. I felt instinctively that this was first of all a piece of music, and I said to Frank, 'It reminds me of the great forgiveness scene at the end of Act IV of *The Marriage of Figaro*, where everyone's singing at the same time.' He smiled and said, 'You've got it.' From that point of view, in performance the scene should feel as though it contains four different worlds happening at exactly the same time in four different locations, and yet those four worlds are somehow speaking across and to each other in one harmoniously discordant fashion.

I worked out the staging in a geometric pattern that grew organically out of the previous scene between The File and William. I wanted a way of creating depth and width, so an audience could feel all four scenes coming at them like pulses through each other part of the scene, so they could see four things at the same time, and hear four things at the same time, plus a choral support that came in from the high balcony. The very fixed visual structure enabled the anarchic language to explode out of it and fill the whole theatre. I knew if I didn't give the scene a very fixed form, the explosions would lack shape and direction and would fall apart under the stress of the scene. The audience had to look from The File and Shakespeare through to Sweney and Maeve, and then from Spenser and Elizabeth through to Ben, Richard and Annas, with Hugh, Donal and Niall framing the scene as they looked down. It was a relationship of angles that I wanted to get.

HL: *My recollection of that scene in your production is that through most of it the women were standing and the men were seated.*

MC: That was a deliberate ploy. It is the women at that moment who are driving the emotional heart of the play, as they always do in a Frank McGuinness play. They are holding the men up. The File is desperately seeking something from Shakespeare, but she is also holding out hope and possibility to him, in many ways. Sexual, but also offering him redemption, allowing him to reconnect with his power, if he will only share it with her. Maeve is desperately trying to keep her king up, who has collapsed Lear-like on the floor and who wants to die, who no longer feels that he has the right or the strength to live or to rule. Maeve tells him, 'You must live to fight.' Annas is offering love to Richard, she is offering to leave her people, her family, everything, and live (as he says) as a whore, in his dirty theatrical world in London. Elizabeth is facing her husband down and saying she will live with him, will die with him, if he will only leave Ireland. So there is this extraordinary passion in all of the women that has an impact on the men, and I wanted to have that felt, with the women standing and the men sitting. There were moments when standing and sitting were reversed, or when Elizabeth came down the stairs. I timed the movements with a balletic quality so a ripple went through the scene.

The visual shape was the easiest thing. Getting the shape, the rhythm of the delivery was hard. The cast were all superb consummate professionals, but you will not find an actor who will gladly walk into a scene that has probably something like 150 one line cues shared by twelve individuals. Your life is too much on the line! Every single night after they warmed up individually they came together to use this scene as a company line call, because they knew it is one of those tunnels that when you are in it you must believe you can reach the end in one piece, together. Frank always asks a great deal of his actors, and no more than in this scene. I set out by directing them to play it without a single pause, at a ferocious, driven pace. I would not say there was resistance, but there was a silent, stunned horror at this command. To be fair they went with me, and they knew at the end that they had something extraordinary to play, which had a huge impact on them every night in the playing. It's a scene in which you are wrapped up, pierced, and overwhelmed by language that comes at such a pace that you don't have a chance to grab any particular moment. You have to let it rush into and through you. Every night, for good or ill, you could feel the intake of breath in the audience. The buttocks would be clenched. They would not move a muscle for these seven minutes or whatever it took, and you could feel the collective heartbeat racing. People sat stunned. It is an astonishing wave of sound.

I believe we have become culturally obsessed by the idea that language is something to be worked out, to be made right, that we've lost the musical, gut quality inherent in its very sound – the aural power of it to affect us physically as a sound wave within which there is meaning. I was influenced in my approach to the scene by Elizabethan composer Thomas Tallis' extraordinary work *Spem in Alium*, which has 40 voices singing across each other, around each other, through each other. Every time I play this piece for people they absolutely know what it is about. They cannot understand it because it is in Latin, but people will talk for hours about what they see and understand from it. They see and hear feelings that they are not getting from the literal meaning of the words but from the musical sound of them. That's what we set out to do in that scene from *Mutabilitie*. To allow words to collide across space, to ricochet off each other, to echo each other. The scene is full of antithesis. We hunted out all the words that echoed each other. One of the breakthroughs for the actors came in rehearsal when I asked what I would regard as the opposite harmonic/discordant couple to play the other scene. They said the lines that were coming at them from another place. Sweney and Maeve got to speak as Shakespeare and The File; Shakespeare and The File got to speak as Sweney and Maeve; and so on. Suddenly the actors understood the impact of the scene as a collective whole. They were not only speaking as their own characters, but they were in some sense reaching behind or above them to the other characters. That's how we bound it together.

HL: *The dinner scene in which the Irish are serving the English is another scene in which power is important.*

MC: As a director there are scenes that tickle your fancy – and they are often the scenes the actors least like at the start of rehearsals. They often seem to revolve around some kind of ritual such as eating, or some kind of formal event. On the page, this mealtime scene is the most dogmatic of all in the play. There's the singing of the great Protestant hymn 'There Is No God but God Alone' at the beginning. Then there's Spenser's lecturing of William on the Irish and their vices, and Elizabeth's counter argument by which she praises the landscape and climate. Not a scene on the page to set an actor on fire. Yet the scene immediately excited me because I felt its power lay in the characters that say not a word, the servants Hugh and File. A scene of contrast between what is being said with the mind, and what is being said by the body. It's one of those fantastic scenes in which a public thing is happening in which the people speaking forget that there are people listening – a scene that becomes rather like a play with a play.

I wanted the audience to be aware that they were watching a great poet and a great aristocrat serve an aspiring poet and aspiring aristocrat. I wanted the issue of power, personal and public, sexual and family, to be the physical sub-text of the language of the scene. The audience had to be watching The File and Hugh, whilst listening to Edmund, his family and their guest William. We explored it from the point of view of what it is like for The File and Hugh to be in that scene, what The File knows about her relationship with William, what Hugh's relationship to William is about, what Hugh's relationship to Spenser is about, what is going on between the File and Hugh at this point in the play. Spenser is oblivious to it all of course. But I staged it so as to let the audience in on the game. The scene became a constant eying up of each other and of pertinent decisions to move. We deliberately choreographed their whole setting of table, and their deliberate placing of objects such as bread and water on it at appropriate moments in the lines, so there was basically an echo going on, a sub-text, that

Spenser was not aware of, but that the audience was. Denis Conway, who played Hugh, played that scene with a tremendous, quiet power. I think he haunted it. He and Liz Schwarz as The File never once broke the boundaries of service, but through their movements and the way they held themselves told us of what it was *really* about.

Emotionally the scene is also important for Spenser's development. A moment that always touched me was when Spenser finds himself under severe emotional stress and his son sings to him the lines from the hymn in an effort to reach out to him across the stage. A contact between son and father is made at last. This sad, cornered man and his young boy trying to join with each other, but they can only do it through singing, not through holding or touching.

It gives such pleasure when a scene like that comes together. When we finished it and when the rest of the cast saw it in run through, people came away saying 'I thought that scene could not be made to work; I did not know why it was there. Now I know *exactly* why it's there. Wow! What a powerful scene.' We knew then we'd got it right.

HL: *McGuinness has described the end of this play as 'ambiguous'. Where, if anywhere, do you find hope in the conclusion?*

MC: Our production ended on a more upbeat tone and note than I believe the original did. I passionately believe that it does have great hope in it. I feel it strongly because I am both Irish and English. This whole issue that has haunted both peoples for so long and sadly still has many miles to go yet before being resolved. I think one of the reasons the play did not do well in England is that there is still abject refusal within English culture to accept the truth of its relationship with the island of Ireland, both in terms of the violence and destruction and also the contradictory love affair that has always existed between the lands. Our two cultures have been intertwined for centuries now and will be forever, so it is vital that we start to look at this relationship with creativity and hope rather than judgment and despair. We need to look into the true heart of our joint stories to recognize that we are far stronger together than apart.

Whenever there is a meal there is hope. Whenever there is a breaking of bread, a sharing of wine, there is hope. Whenever people can sit down and do the most basic, natural human things together, there is hope. Yes Niall and Donal (the priest) are standing in the background watching as Hugh, The File, and Annas sit with the English boy and give him their food. But it is Hugh, The File, and Annas that hold the power. In the great, great scene that precedes it, the family is forced to accept its guilt. Hugh acknowledges that in killing his own parents, his ancient past, he has also killed his right to retributional judgement of others, for by his actions and the actions of his tribe, he is as much to blame as anyone for the pain that is now in the play. He has become that great Shakespearean concept – 'nothing'. He frees himself of his ego and becomes a child wandering through the forest. When the child is found, the threat of violence rears its ugly head once more. We worked hard to create the sense of Niall and Donal circling the child like hunters preparing the act of sacrifice, preparing the act of brutality. That desire was there in the scene. Just before they sit down to eat, it looks as though they are going to do harm to the child. Annas says 'We have a child', and Niall cries out 'An English child', and Donal, 'A hostage!' to which Hugh responds emphatically 'We have a child!' I've just become a father. You think you know it before, but when you have a child you *really* know that every child, whatever race, whatever colour or creed, comes into this world a pure thing. If we learned more from our relationship to our own childhood and to children in general, we would perhaps produce a better world. That's why Hugh's answer to Donal is so important: 'We have a child!' A child does not become a dogma or an ideology or a part of a nation until we have corrupted it. The purity of a child must always be recognized, because it's about possibility.

Hugh is given a choice when he meets this physical child. It's like re-meeting his soul, and the strange thing is that the soul is an English boy. They sit down together, and there are the simple words, 'There is milk.' The priest tries to say, 'There is little', but The File says, 'Fetch our little milk. Drink the milk. Eat.' And the child eats and drinks. They then all eat together. I believe the whole purpose, the whole balance of the play is disturbed if you stage this scene without favouring hope. Yes, with Donal and Niall at the edge, weapon in hand, watching, there is still danger, but the real power and beauty lies in the sight of a man and a woman who have lost a child sitting down with the child of their enemy and sharing the last food and drink that they have. The milk of human kindness.

We have too much cynicism in our world, too much reaching into easy platitudes and over simplified interpretations of history in an effort to justify all kinds of brutalities. The play is about the fact that each has done so much to the other and it is now time to move forward. It is important that we say that loud and clear –not forgetting the past, but not obsessing about it either. The sight of a child sitting down and eating is about the future.

HL: *If you were required to say in a few words what* Mutabilitie *is about, what would you say?*

MC: In the simplest terms, *Mutabilitie* is about the fundamental truth that the secret to life is about accepting change. The universe is apparently fixed and yet at the very same time it is free. There are constants that will one day change. Everything that is born must pass into the darkness if there is to be new life. All our visions of ourselves will change into something else in the future. It was inevitable that England and Ireland would have a history. It was inevitable that that history would involve things that brought sadness and joy. Many things would change that many people desperately wanted to hold on to. However, until you accept this fact of life you will not be able to accept the lives of others, you will not accept the fact that life is a process of give and take and flow. The goddess Mutabilitie still sits on the hill and says, 'What are you blaming me for? Without me you cannot exist. Without change you cannot have any constancy.' The play speaks of this truth from a political point of view, a historical point of view, from a sexual point of view, from an emotional point of view, from a personal point of view. That's a theology, an idea of life that most people struggle with because it's so frightening. When people see their nearest and dearest murdered, their culture raped, they want someone else to pay for it. It asks a lot to say, 'This has happened, we are alive. What are we going to create out of this change? Possibility or more pain?'

The play is begging two cultures, two races, to move forward, with the past, but accepting and embracing the changes that have happened. For all of the pain and all of the terror, we are both responsible and we are both changed. That change has possibilities and hope for the future.

HL: Did post-colonial theory or gender studies have an impact on how you approached the play?

MC: As a maker of theatre I don't let myself worry about that kind of thing. I was obviously very, very personally aware of post-colonial issues. You can't have my very English accent and live in Ireland and not be aware of the post-colonial environment in which you live and what it means to the Irish collective unconscious. Thus I would approach such theory from a standpoint of personal understanding rather than intellectual exploration. I did not want to read points of view. I have absorbed a lot from ten years of living in Ireland. The post-colonial experience was very much in the production room, because it could not fail to be; we had a cast that was primarily Irish, but with several English actors as well. For everyone there was a journey. At times very strong points of view came up, differences between the two cultures came to the fore. There was never anything other than great camaraderie, but the experience of being a post-colonial nation with the colonizer in the rehearsal room produced important debate. It brought the play home. Irish actors would jokingly refer to other Irish actors playing English characters as 'turncoats' and 'informers.' Then they would have to recognize what they were doing by this. The actors had to absorb the fact that this was not a play about who was right and who was wrong. It's a play about experiencing the totality of colonial experience, for both the colonized and the colonizer. In England there is still a failure to grasp this duality of experience, to see that the experience of being a colonizer has brutalized them to. That is why they are so frightened of any kind of perceived assault on the upright pillars of their culture, in particular William Shakespeare. The idea that William Shakespeare was gay or at least bi-sexual, that still remains an absolute no-no in so many quarters. But far worse would be to suggest, as Frank does, the tainting of his creativity by a influential visit – real or imagined – to another culture, particularly Ireland.

One of the scenes important to me is in Act Two, when The File and Shakespeare, shall we say, conceive Sonnet 18. That was one scene that Frank and I spent some time on. In the original draft it was very clear that The File was offering lines to William. He was struggling to make the connections, and she would give him various phrases. In the printed version, William speaks almost the whole sonnet. I asked Frank to let me return to his original idea; that William is making the sonnet, but The File has shared moments of creative influence and helps him shape it. As William grows into the sonnet he is leaning on The File for support. She as a great creative talent offers him little moments that help make the connections he is reaching for. So the sonnet in some sense is a collaboration. I think a number of English members of our audience found that scene very difficult to take: the idea that someone else would come between the Holy Bard and his great force. Other people were astonished by the idea, which gave great tangibility to the brilliant tradition of the bards of Ireland (as well as the likes of Shakespeare being but a continuation of this ancient, Shamanic line) and also to the idea Frank's playing with – the bringing of Shakespeare to Ireland to re-release this creative force within modern Irish poets. You're always going to upset people when you step on holy icons and suggest that they're not the way they are perceived. One of the things I love about this play is the way Shakespeare is presented. He's an extraordinary creation, ambiguous, contradictory, troubled. Able to be one thing one minute and another, another. Driven by some ferocious gift that he has almost no control of. The greatest theatrical, the greatest poetic maestro of the ages and obviously a huge influence on Frank.

In terms of gender, it was only an issue in terms of the acting of the play. The female characters tower over it, equal and impressive. The actresses were all powerful forces in their own right. Rarely have I had the pleasure of working in a room in which the balance of power between the genders was so evenly matched. No theory needed to take place here. Just hard sweat and tears from all.

HL: *What McGuinness play would you like to direct next?*

MC: A new one please, Frank! No seriously, there's nothing more enticing than directing a new piece. One reason doing *Mutabilitie* was so exciting is that in many ways it was a new play from an Irish point of view. Other than that, probably *Innocence*, though I've a deep love for *Carthaginians*, which I directed with a student cast from New York University. I've been surprised there has not been a production of *Carthaginians* in a front line theatre in the Republic for the last few years, considering everything that's happened of late in the North, including the ongoing Bloody Sunday inquest. But maybe that's exactly why it hasn't happened.

HL: *What qualities in a director help when approaching a McGuinness play?*

MC: You have to love the imagination. You have to be driven by a desire to produce poetic drama. You've got to be able to balance flow and sharp edges. Frank's plays are not comfortable. They have great form. They have wonderful sweep. They have tremendous energy, and it's easy to see them glide across the page and across the stage. But there are these stunning, staccato punches that come up underneath the through-line of the play. Moments or lines or characters that just barge their way into the text. You must never try and quieten these moments. Try and make them fit. Like fire crackers, they are just best set off. You've also got to be willing to take risks with his work. Not try to limit it, but set it free. Allow it to be beautiful and ugly at the same time. The trial scene in *Mutabilitie* is a truly ugly scene and should be disturbing and upsetting. It comes on the back of a moment when the play appears to give the Irish justification for all of their hurt and pain. Suddenly we see them acting in a truly barbaric fashion. You could easily try and hide that scene, tame it, but you've got to be willing to say Frank is putting *everything* on the stage, warts and all, and it's important to really show the warts. Something about the visceral, physical urgency of the man himself comes through in these moments.

And you've got to completely understand the concept of the Other. You've got to be driven by the idea that Frank takes Outsiders – whether they're Outsiders because of their culture or because of their personal sexual culture as gay men – and understand that they are engines of change. Because they are not at the centre and trapped by the centre, they are free. Things that are fixed need something uncomfortable and jagged and dangerous to break them free. Dido in *Carthaginians* is a classic example. He is not a figure of fun. Like a true clown he is a dark and sad figure as well as a gloriously funny one. He has a tremendous vitality that is unsettling as well as joyful. It's important never to make Frank's characters smooth.

HL: *It often strikes me that McGuinness's Outsiders, Dido and others – if they survive – have learned strategies for coping with difficulties in the world that face all of us. These Outsiders, then, function as role models for those less outside, providing clues for survival in this dangerous, glorious world.*

MC: Exactly. Those moments in *Mutabilitie* where sexual lines are crossed are those moments when characters reach into their true hearts and are truly honest with themselves or someone else for the first time. They're not playing sexual games for advantage; they're caught in a fuller apprehension of themselves. It happens to Hugh, it happens to The File in the great love scene when the two men and the two women find themselves close to a homosexual or lesbian moment. It releases them in a sense. I think Frank sees that liberty as a creative force for good. People are enabled to break through because they've seen something that otherwise they wouldn't have seen.

HL: *How would you position McGuinness in relationship to the rest of contemporary Irish drama?*

MC: I believe Frank McGuinness is one of the most important playwrights working in the world today. I believe his canon will have longevity greater than that of some playwrights who at the moment enjoy greater public awareness and acclaim. Something about it transcends the time and place it was written in. *Carthaginians* will be played in 400 years time and felt in the same way it is felt today; it will not date. I believe *Mutabilitie* will come in to its own in future years as others realize its greatness, as it breaks free of the particular limitations set by contemporary culture. I do not think McGuinness is a contemporary playwright. His greatness is that his plays feel very ancient and very forward, very future. Along with people like Marina Carr he is one of the last voices that is writing theatre of imagination and poetry and metaphysics. He creates a theatrical experience that transcends the normal. I hope and believe that the best is still to come. He's still a young writer, a ferociously active writer of great passion. I look forward with great anticipation, always, to the next Frank McGuinness play.

Contributors

Margot Gayle Backus is Associate Professor of English at the University of Houston. She has published numerous articles on topics ranging from American lesbian elegy to Irish film. Her book, *The Gothic Family Romance: Heterosexuality, Child Sacrifice and the Anglo-Irish Colonial Order* (Duke UP) was published in 1999. She is currently researching a book on masculinity at the margins of British national identity.

Sharon Braden has a Master of Arts degree from the University of Hawaii and is a Ph.D. candidate in Dramatic Arts at the University of California, Davis. She performs, directs, and teaches a variety of theatre and dramatic courses. Her dissertation, 'Re-mapping the Island of Ireland: Social and Political Space in Contemporary Irish Performance', will be completed in spring 2003.

Brian Cliff is currently a Brittain Teaching Fellow at the Georgia Institute of Technology (Atlanta). In 2001-2002, he was a Visiting Assistant Professor at Emory University, where he completed his Ph.D. He has given papers on a range of Irish authors, including Douglas Hyde, J.M. Synge, Frank McGuinness, Paul Muldoon, and Patrick McCabe, and has published on the publicity for the Irish Literary Theatre. His present project examines approaches to community in contemporary Irish literature.

Timothy D. Connors is Professor of Theatre at Central Michigan University, where he teaches a variety of performance and academic courses. He has also held teaching and administrative positions in Arizona and Texas. In addition to Irish theatre and drama, Connors maintains research interests in American vaudeville and burlesque, late nineteenth and early twentieth century American theatre and drama, and Soviet and Polish theatre and drama. He is an active director with a special interest in new plays.

Joan FitzPatrick Dean is Professor of English at the University of Missouri-Kansas City. In 1992-93 she was Fulbright Scholar at University College Galway and in 1982-83 Fulbright Lecturer at Université de Nancy in France. Her publications on Irish and British drama include 'Tom Stoppard: Comedy as a Moral Matrix', the forthcoming *Ireland into Film* volume on 'Dancing at Lughnasa', and articles in *New Hibernia Review*, *Modern Drama, Nua, Theatre Journal*, and *Theatre Survey*.

Kathleen Heininge received her Master of Arts from California State University, Hayward, having worked on Yeats, Ibsen, and the establishment of national theatres. She received her doctorate from University of California, Davis, with a dissertation entitled "The Broth of a Boy': Manifestations of the Stage Irish Figure in 20th Century Irish Drama.' Articles on Frank McGuinness, Stephen King, and Terry McMillan are forthcoming, and she is preparing her dissertation for publication and writing a play.

Eamonn Jordan is a lecturer in Drama at the Institute of Technology Sligo. His Ph. D. (1994) on the dramas of Frank McGuinness is re-worked as *The Feast of Famine: The Plays of Frank McGuinness* (Bern: Peter Lang, 1997). He is the editor of *Theatre Stuff: Critical Essays on Contemporary Irish Theatre* (Dublin: Carysfort Press, 2000) and is a co-editor of *Theatre Talk: Voices of Irish Theatre Practitioners* (Dublin: Carysfort Press, 2001). He has written *Someone Who'll Watch Over Me: A Critical Commentary* (Dublin: CJ Fallon Educational Publishers, 2000). He has published a number of essays on contemporary Irish Theatre in journals and edited collections.

Anne F. Kelly-O'Reilly is a lecturer in the Religious Studies Department at St. Patrick's College, Drumcondra, Dublin. Her areas of interest include feminist philosophy, spirituality, literature and the sacred. She was co-editor of *Womanspirit: The Irish journal of feminist spirituality*. She is completing a doctorate and writing a book on Soul Journeys in Contemporary Irish Drama. Recent publications include 'Bodies and Spirits in Tom Murphy's Theatre' in *Theatre Stuff: Critical Essays on Contemporary Irish Drama* (Carysfort Press, 2000).

Helen Lojek is Professor of English at Boise State University (Idaho). Her publications on Irish drama have appeared in *Irish University Review, Éire-Ireland, Contemporary Literature, Modern Drama, New Hibernia Review, Canadian Journal of Irish Studies. Contexts for Frank McGuinness's Drama* is forthcoming from Catholic University Press.

Christopher Murray is Associate Professor of Drama and Theatre History at University College Dublin. He is author of *Twentieth-Century Irish Drama: Mirror Up to Nation* (1997) and is currently working on a biography of Sean O'Casey.

Bernice Schrank is Professor of English at Memorial University of Newfoundland, Canada. She publishes extensively on Irish literature, in particular on the dramatic works of Sean O'Casey, Brendan Behan, Brian Friel, and Frank McGuinness. Her latest book, *Sean O'Casey: A Research and Production Sourcebook*, was published by Greenwood Press.

Carysfort Press was formed in the summer of 1998. It receives annual funding from the Arts Council.

The directors believe that drama is playing an ever-increasing role in today's society and that enjoyment of the theatre, both professional and amateur, currently plays a central part in Irish culture.

The Press aims to produce high quality publications which, though written and/or edited by academics, will be made accessible to a general readership. The organisation would also like to provide a forum for critical thinking in the Arts in Ireland, again keeping the needs and interests of the general public in view.

The company publishes contemporary Irish writing for and about the theatre.

Editorial and publishing inquiries to:
CARYSFORT PRESS
58 Woodfield, Scholarstown Road,
Rathfarnham, Dublin 16,
Republic of Ireland
T (353 1) 493 7383 F (353 1) 406 9815
e: info@carysfortpress.com
www.carysfortpress.com

NEW TITLES

GEORG BÜCHNER: WOYZECK
A NEW TRANSLATION
BY DAN FARRELLY

The most up-to-date German scholarship of Thomas Michael Mayer and Burghard Dedner has finally made it possible to establish an authentic sequence of scenes. The wide-spread view that this play is a prime example of loose, open theatre is no longer sustainable.   Directors and teachers are challenged   to "read it again".

ISBN 1-904505-02-3
€18

THE THEATRE OF FRANK MCGUINNESS
STAGES OF MUTABILITY
BY HELEN LOJEK

The first edited collection of essays about internationally renowned Irish playwright Frank McGuinness focuses on both performance and text. Interpreters come to diverse conclusions, creating a vigorous dialogue that enriches understanding and reflects a strong consensus about the value of McGuinness's complex work.

ISBN 1-904505-01-5
€15

NEW TITLES

THE THEATRE OF MARINA CARR
"BEFORE RULES WAS MADE"
EDITED BY ANNA MCMULLAN
& CATHY LEENEY

As the first published collection of articles on the theatre of Marina Carr, this volume explores the world of Carr's theatrical imagination, the place of her plays in comtemporary theatre in Ireland and abroad and the significance of her highly individual voice.

ISBN 0-9534-2577-0
€15

TALKING ABOUT TOM MURPHY
EDITED BY NICHOLAS GRENE

Talking About Tom Murphy is shaped around the six plays in the landmark Abbey Theatre Murphy Season of 2001, assembling some of the best-known commentators on his work: Fintan O'Toole, Chris Morash, Lionel Pilkington, Alexandra Poulain, Shaun Richards, Nicholas Grene and Declan Kiberd.

ISBN 0-9534-2579-7
€10

HAMLET
THE SHAKESPEAREAN DIRECTOR
BY MIKE WILCOCK

"This study of the Shakespearean director as viewed through various interpretations of HAMLET is a welcome addition to our understanding of how essential it is for a director to have a clear vision of a great play. It is an important study from which all of us who love Shakespeare and who understand the importance of continuing contemporary exploration may gain new insights."

From the Foreword, by Joe Dowling, Artistic Director, The Guthrie Theater, Minneapolis, MN

ISBN 1-904505-00-7
€18

THEATRE OF SOUND
RADIO AND THE
DRAMATIC IMAGINATION
BY DERMOT RATTIGAN

An innovative study of the challenges that radio drama poses to the creative imagination of the writer, the production team, and the listener.

"A remarkably fine study of radio drama – everywhere informed by the writer's professional experience of such drama in the making... A new theoretical and analytical approach – informative, illuminating and at all times readable.'

Richard Allen Cave

ISBN 0-9534-2575-4
€20

BACK LIST

THEATRE TALK
VOICES OF IRISH THEATRE PRACTITIONERS
EDITED BY LILIAN CHAMBERS, GER FITZGIBBON & EAMONN JORDAN

"This book is the right approach - asking practitioners what they feel."
Sebastian Barry, Playwright.

"... an invaluable and informative collection of interviews with those who make and shape the landscape of Irish Theatre."
Ben Barnes, Artistic Director of the Abbey Theatre

ISBN 0-9534-2576-2
€20

IN SEARCH OF THE SOUTH AFRICAN IPHIGENIE
BY ERIKA VON WIETERSHEIM AND DAN FARRELLY

Discussions of Goethe's "Iphigenie auf Tauris" (Under the Curse) as relevant to women's issues in modern South Africa: women in family and public life; the force of women's spirituality; experience of personal relationships; attitudes to parents and ancestors; involvement with religion.

ISBN 0-9534-2578-9
€10

THE STARVING AND OCTOBER SONG
TWO CONTEMPORARY IRISH PLAYS
BY ANDREW HINDS

The Starving, set during and after the siege of Derry in 1689, is a moving and engrossing drama of the emotional journey of two men.

October Song, a superbly written family drama set in real time in pre-ceasefire Derry.

ISBN 0-9534-2574-6
€10

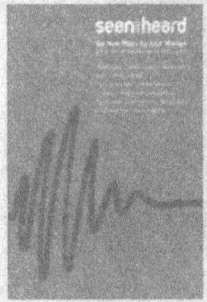

SEEN AND HEARD (REPRINT)
SIX NEW PLAYS BY IRISH WOMEN
EDITED WITH AN INTRODUCTION BY CATHY LEENEY

A rich and funny, moving and theatrically exciting collection of plays by Mary Elizabeth Burke-Kennedy, Siofra Campbell, Emma Donoghue, Anne Le Marquand Hartigan, Michelle Read and Dolores Walshe.

ISBN 0-9534-2573-8
€20

BACK LIST

THEATRE STUFF (REPRINT)
CRITICAL ESSAYS ON CONTEMPORARY IRISH THEATRE
EDITED BY EAMONN JORDAN

Best selling essays on the successes and debates of contemporary Irish theatre at home and abroad.

Contributors include: Thomas Kilroy, Declan Hughes, Anna McMullan, Declan Kiberd, Deirdre Mulrooney, Fintan O'Toole, Christopher Murray, Caoimhe McAvinchey and Terry Eagleton.

ISBN 0-9534-2571-1
€19

URFAUST
A NEW VERSION OF GOETHE'S EARLY "FAUST" IN BRECHTIAN MODE
BY DAN FARRELLY

This version is based on Brecht's irreverent and daring re-interpretation of the German classic.

"Urfaust is a kind of well-spring for German theatre... The love-story is the most daring and the most profound in German dramatic literature." *Brecht*

ISBN 0-9534257-0-3
€7.60

UNDER THE CURSE
GOETHE'S "IPHIGENIE AUF TAURIS", IN A NEW VERSION
BY DAN FARRELLY

The Greek myth of Iphigenie grappling with the curse on the house of Atreus is brought vividly to life. This version is currently being used in Johannesburg to explore problems of ancestry, religion, and Black African women's spirituality.

ISBN 0-9534-2572-X
€20

HOW TO ORDER
TRADE ORDERS DIRECTLY TO

CMD
Columba Mercier Distribution
55A Spruce Avenue
Stillorgan Industrial Park
Blackrock
Co. Dublin

T (353 1) 294 2560
F (353 1) 294 2564
E cmd@columba.ie

or contact
SALES@BROOKSIDE.IE

www.ingramcontent.com/pod-product-compliance
Lightning Source LLC
Chambersburg PA
CBHW070326230426
43663CB00011B/2236